Praise for
*Innovation for*
*the Fatigued*

'More than ever, innovation has become a prime success factor, yet we all have experienced some kind of fatigue as the term has become a cliché. In this book, Alf Rehn looks critically at the evolution of innovation practices throughout the past decades and teaches us new techniques on how to embrace innovation 4.0. An absolute must-read for anyone who wants to succeed, or just survive, in today's world.'
ANTONIO NIETO-RODRIGUEZ, AUTHOR OF *THE PROJECT REVOLUTION* AND *THE FOCUSED ORGANIZATION*, AND NAMED WORLD'S LEADING CHAMPION OF PROJECT MANAGEMENT BY THINKERS50

'Some innovation is a quick fix, some takes a lifetime of dedication. Some new ideas are new products or services, while other new ideas bring revolutions in the way people live or think. In this important book, Alf Rehn urges leaders to reject wasteful stereotypes of creativity and to embrace the truths needed to deliver powerful real-world innovation. If innovation is deviance in practice, then Rehn is a most practical deviant.'
DR MAX MCKEOWN, AUTHOR OF *THE INNOVATION BOOK*

'Now that the global innovation hype bubble is bursting, the world desperately needs a dose of straight talk. It's time the clichés were put up against the wall and out of their misery. Alf Rehn brings his no-nonsense, shelve-the-bullshit style to this refreshing reset on what innovation is, what it can do, and how organizations might finally realize its value. He shows innovation isn't just about desire or a popular process, but requires deeper cultural intervention and an embedded mindset.'
SCOTT SMITH, WORLD-LEADING FUTURIST AND FOUNDER OF CHANGEIST

# Innovation for the Fatigued

*How to build a culture of deep creativity*

Alf Rehn

**KoganPage**

First published in Great Britain and the United States in 2019 by Kogan Page Limited

2nd Floor, 45 Gee Street
London
EC1V 3RS
United Kingdom
www.koganpage.com

122 W 27th St, 10th Floor
New York, NY 10001
USA

4737/23 Ansari Road
Daryaganj
New Delhi 110002
India

**ISBNs**

HARDBACK     978 0 7494 9800 9
PAPERBACK    978 0 7494 8408 8
E-ISBN       978 0 7494 8409 5

**British Library Cataloguing-in-Publication Data**

A CIP record for this book is available from the British Library

**Library of Congress Cataloging-in-Publication Data**
Names: Rehn, Alf, author.
Title: Innovation for the fatigued : how to build a culture of deep creativity / Alf Rehn.
Description: London ; New York : Kogan Page Limited, 2019. | Includes bibliographical references and index.
Identifiers: LCCN 2018058151 (print) | LCCN 2019000013 (ebook) | ISBN 9780749484095 (E-book) | ISBN 9780749498009 (hardback) | ISBN 9780749484088 (pbk.)
Subjects: LCSH: Creative ability in business. | Creative thinking. | Technological innovations. | Corporate culture.
Classification: LCC HD53 (ebook) | LCC HD53 .R4195 2019 (print) | DDC 658.3/14—dc23

Typeset by Integra Software Services, Pondicherry
Print production managed by Jellyfish
Printed and bound by CPI Group (UK) Ltd, Croydon CR0 4YY

# Contents

# Acknowledgements

This book has something of an intricate history. It has, at various times, been a critical diatribe on innovation, a manifesto for better innovation and an analysis of innovation discourses. Before it took the form you have before you, it has existed as at least two unfinished manuscripts and one published book. As a result, there are far too many people to acknowledge, and I will not even attempt such a list. Instead, I will keep it short and sweet.

I would like to thank Géraldine Collard, who commissioned the book and made me believe that writing it would be a meaningful project. I would also like to thank my editor, Christopher Cudmore, who managed to curb some of my authorial excesses and gently encouraged me in the process, all whilst fretting over my cavalier attitude towards deadlines. I would also like to give a shoutout (as the young folks call it) to Marcus Lindahl, Ann Rippin, Karoline Kjellstedt, Anders Jensen, Niclas Lindgren and all my other friends who had to deal with or work around my, at times, lackadaisical focus and attention.

Most of all I want to thank my nearest and dearest. My older children, Sean and Line Rehn, both became adults (or a reasonable facsimile thereof) during the process of writing this book. My youngest child, the Noëlskinator (aka Noël Muhr Rehn), has often interrupted the writing of this by insisting we do something more important, like get ice cream or play Bloons or Fortnite. All of them deserve my most heartfelt thanks.

My fondest and warmest thanks goes to my beloved partner Kate Hodsdon, who has been unwavering in her support as well as gracious in suffering the many pains having a writer as a partner can bring. She has been ever-present in the writing of this, and it is only fair to say the book exists because of her.

*We live in a business world that increasingly worships the great tribal god innovation, lyrically hailing it not just as a desired, but as a necessary, condition of a company's survival and growth. This highly agitated confidence in the liberating efficacy of innovation has in some places become an article of faith almost as strong as the Natchez Indian's consuming faith in the deity of the sun. Man creates gods according to his needs. Significantly, the businessman's new demigod and the Natchez's more venerable and historic god make identical promises. They both promise renewal and life.*

*Theodore Levitt in 'Innovative imitation',*
Harvard Business Review, *September 1966*

# CHAPTER ONE

# Introduction

*Between the shallows and the deep blue sea*

'*As the births of living creatures are at first ill-shapen, so are all innovations, which are the births of time.*' FRANCIS BACON

## Scenes from our innovation crisis

This is a book about innovation cultures and about why some cultures can engage with innovation on a deep level, whilst others get stuck in the shallow and superficial. But it is also a book with a warning. Despite the talk about innovation, despite the professed love for it, there is a lurking crisis at the heart of it all. A crisis that can be intimated from things both big and small. We shall start with the latter.

*Scene 1*: The year is 2006, and I am a young, fresh-faced professor. I got tenure and a chair a few years previously, and I do have some experience in working with corporations. I have just arrived at the headquarters of a major such, and have been led to a large seminar room in which 100+ people sit and wait. The preamble has been dealt with, and I am introduced. I step up in front of the crowd and say 'Hello! My name is Alf Rehn, and I am here to help you with your innovation initiative'.

The reaction is as immediate as it is positive. People smile, if sometimes just slightly, and you can notice a fair few people expectantly sitting up a little straighter. Some eyes twinkle, and not just from amusement. In the discussion that follows it becomes evident that people are enthusiastic about the idea of trying out new things, breaking old barriers and the like. This enthusiasm isn't necessarily evenly shared, but it is there.

*Scene 2*: The year is 2018, and I am no longer quite as young. I am, however, very experienced when it comes to working on creativity and innovation in corporations. I arrive at the head-quarters of a corporation much like the one in scene 1. I am led into a seminar room also very much like the one in the first scene, both when it comes to the look of the room and the look of the people gathered within it. The preamble is noticeably similar, as is my opening line: 'Hello! My name is Alf Rehn, and I am here to help you with your innovation initiative'.

What follows, though, is markedly different. The smiles are still there, and there are many in the room who are clearly excited about it all. But it is no longer universal. Amongst the smiles are also looks of exhaustion and exasperation. Some in the audience look down-right dejected. In fact, I can hear a person muttering 'Oh no, not this again'.

I do not offer these scenes as proof that I've become markedly duller over the years. In fact, I often achieve better results in corporations now than I did 12 years ago. What I offer in these scenes might best be described as an insight into what has happened with innovation since the late 2000s. As the term went from battle cry to buzzword, and organization after organiza-tion started hunting for it in increasingly desperate ways, the manner in which innovation is understood and received under-went a transformation, and not always a happy one at that.

Whereas innovation is universally hailed as a critical business competence, the literal thing that organizations need to survive and succeed, it has also become something of a pain. In the mid-2000s, you might find the occasional larger organization that didn't run a yearly innovation initiative, or that didn't have an idea competition or recurring workshops on business model innovation. Today, they're rarer than unicorns (both the startup and the horses with a horn kind). In the mid-2000s, a new innovation book was an interesting addition to the canon. Today, it's frequently grist for the mill.

In a contemporary organization, the average employee has heard the term bandied about more times than they can count, seen numerous innovation consultants pass through, developed a slight allergy to multi-coloured Post-it® notes, and feel, on the whole, sick and tired of it all. The audience in my second scene wasn't sick of me. Instead, they were suffering from *innovation fatigue*. It is a curious illness, this, being exhausted by that which was supposed to energize. But right now, it is a rapidly spreading malaise, and it's evolving towards a pandemic – even as we move towards an imagination economy. It is an illness that is brought on by a peculiar and insidious process, one where innovation moved away from being a powerful change agent and instead became something... different. Something... shallow.

This is a book about this challenge. It is a book about how innovation became something shallow and superficial, and what we can do about it. It is a book about the enormous potential society and organizations have to innovate and what needs to be done to capture it. It is a book about how vapid and empty sloganeering took over innovation thinking and about how we can fight back. It is about going deep; about crafting deeper innovation cultures, about rediscovering innovation ambition, about going deep into diversity. But most of all it is about ideas and humans and the need to save both from the shallows that are much of modern innovation thinking.

## An age of innovation talk

Have you ever sat in on an innovation workshop and seminar and had the sensation that you've heard it all before? The terminology starts to blur, and you can't even remember if there's a difference between disruptive and transformative. You also can't remember when it became acceptable to describe a new way to sell coffee, or empty a rubbish bin, as being radical or revolutionary. You look at the slides, and somehow every example is giving you a massive feeling of déjà vu. That is, until you realize that it isn't déjà vu, not really, you just literally have heard it all before. You used to like Elon Musk, but now there's a tiny twitch in your eye when either he or Tesla gets mentioned. Congratulations, you've experienced *shallow innovation.*

*Congratulations, you've experienced shallow innovation.*

This year, like every year for the last few ones, more than 100 books on innovation will be published *every month.*[1] Not all of them will be on innovation management in companies, and some might have a somewhat tangential connection to the theme, but this is what you can gather if you go through publishing data and see how books are categorized on platforms such as Google Books and Amazon – more than 100 books a month. That means that if you read three books on innovation a day, you're actually falling behind. And this is just the books. To this comes a plethora of other material, an unending tsunami of LinkedIn-content, magazines, Twitter-feeds, blogs and sundry government pamphlets. We may need to have a discussion regarding how innovative our age really is, but one thing is true beyond any doubt:

**We live in the golden age of innovation chatter!**

But whilst there is lots of talk, we should perhaps pause for a moment and ask what is really being said in this torrent of words and pictures. Is all this talk really making organizations more creative and society more innovative? Or is it all just... talk? I'm a professor of innovation (more to the point, I'm the professor of innovation, design and management at the faculty of engineering at SDU in Denmark), so talk and text about innovation are pretty much what I do all day, every day. Those 100 books? I'm the guy who is supposed to keep up with it all, and although I cannot claim I read three innovation books a day, I read a lot of them. I can thus tell you what would happen to you if you actually tried to read all that is written about innovation. You would go insane, but not for the reasons people might think. You see, reading the innovation literature of today doesn't put you at risk of having your mind blown. Instead, you'd go crazy from the sheer *boredom* of it all.

Why? Because for all the talk about revolutions and 'thinking outside the box' (a phrase I hate with such a burning passion I would like for it to be outlawed), the most pressing characteristic of contemporary innovation literature is how maddeningly similar and repetitive it is. The advice given is so standardized it cannot be more than a year or so until an AI can write an innovation book, using the same, endlessly repeated advice: look outside your industry for ideas, listen to diverse groups of people, experiment and test with customers, take chances, learn to love failure. See, I just saved you from reading 50 of the best-selling innovation books published since the early 2010s. *You're welcome.* If the advice is standardized, that's still nothing compared to the examples and cases. I used to joke that there seemingly was a law that said each innovation book needed to reference Apple before page 10, or the book would be pulled from circulation. Today, of course, things have changed. Now you have to mention both Apple *and* Tesla before page 10...

Joking aside, the number of companies that are endlessly referenced and re-referenced in the innovation literature makes for a rather depressing list: Apple, Airbnb, Amazon, Google, Facebook, Netflix and Tesla. Rinse and repeat. Once in a while someone sneaks in some lesser known company, but the tendency is clear. The same can also be seen in the often quite tragic lists of 'The World's Most Innovative Companies' that magazines often devote ink and bandwidth to. Gary Lineker, the UK football pundit, famously described football as being 'a simple game. Twenty-two men chase a ball for 90 minutes and at the end, the Germans always win'.[2] Today, we might say that innovation is an astoundingly complex phenomenon, but when listing the most innovative companies, Apple always wins. In late 2014, two competing consulting companies, Boston Consulting Group and Strategy& (the consulting arm of PwC) published independent reports purporting to make clear once and for all which were the world's most innovative companies.[3] The former listed the top three as Apple, Google and Samsung. The latter's list was Apple, Google and Amazon. Looking at both lists, the top 10 were 70 per cent identical, if with slightly shuffled positions. Fast forward to 2018, and Fast Company's list of *The 50 Most Innovative Companies in the World*,[4] and the only thing that has truly changed is that Google has fallen out of favour – but Apple still holds #1 with Amazon at #5. The more things change...

*Innovation talk isn't really about innovation. In fact, a lot of innovation isn't about innovation.*

What is going on here? In a word, innovation talk isn't really about innovation. In fact, a lot of innovation isn't about innovation. As a result, we need to start to have a serious talk about what innovation is today and about the difference between shallow and deep innovation thinking.

## Innovation ain't what it used to be

Innovation used to be a term used sparingly for a limited number of clearly defined projects. Today, the term is used for nigh on everything, from the most minute improvement of an existing product to truly revolutionary developments – and many things besides. In my work with innovation I've often come across uses of the word that might seem humorous, until you understand how problematic they are. The CEO of Kellogg's famously declared that the introduction of a new flavour (peanut butter!) to Pop-Tarts, a product that has existed for over 50 years, counted as an innovation. This got even the *Wall Street Journal*, not known for their aversion to business hyperbole, to publish a most sarcastic rebuttal.[5] I have seen pencil sharpeners advertised as 'revolutionary' innovations in classroom technology[6] and the most traditional of people claiming themselves to be innovators or innovation mavens, and you can probably add several other examples of nonsensical uses of the word. In fact, the manner in which innovation has become the go-to description of nigh on everything is today such a universal phenomenon that few of us even react any longer. Innovation, and the various words associated with it – creativity, revolution, disruption and so on – has become the business equivalent of elevator music. We don't really listen, yet we expect it to be there.

It doesn't take a genius to realize that this also comes at a cost. The aforementioned tsunami of innovation talk, coupled with the contemporary tendency to call everything and thereby nothing innovation, has created an environment in which innovation fatigue is a completely normal reaction.[7] It isn't that people don't want to innovate; of course they do. But as what they get served is less a discussion about solving meaningful problems and more about recycled and regurgitated clichés, people tire. And with clichéd innovation talk comes other ills. As innovation talk has become more and more superficial, we have started seeing a narrowing of innovation thinking, one where people look more to how they can repeat whatever buzzword is beloved at the moment – be it gamification, open innovation, freemium as a business model, or trying to get in on the AI craze – than what impact they might achieve.

I have taken to calling this 'shallow innovation'. For most people, it's just innovation as usual, or the normal way of talking about innovation, but this is because we've not talked enough about the alternatives to it and the critique it should be subjected to. Shallow innovation is a way of engaging with innovation that emphasizes style over substance and easily recognizable stories over stories that might actually drive innovation forwards. It cares more about fitting in with today's narrative than breaking truly new ground, and it dominates not only the literature but also companies.

## Scenes from a shallow company

The greatest thing I ever wrote, something I've jokingly referred to as my *magnum opus*, was a 20-minute lecture on innovation for the executive team of a major US corporation. As they do not come out all that well in this story, I won't use their name, but if you are a modern individual, you will have worked with their products. They are a major player in the broad field of IT and electronics, and are often highlighted when you look for the most innovative companies in the world. And no, it's not Apple.

I was approached by this company off the back of a very successful keynote speech at a major tech conference, to run a two-day workshop for them. At first, I planned to say no. They were simply too big, too imposing, too successful for me to dare run anything for them. I was, in a word, scared of them. I have tangled with the big boys, but this was something more. This was using two whole days to tell some of the most successful innovators in the world about innovation, and I was deathly afraid that I'd come away from it looking like a fool.

I have my pride, so I prepared extremely well. In fact, I estimated I had prepared enough material for a five-day workshop, partly because it might be handy to have, partly because it ensured I would always have more material in case my audience started protesting. I flew out to the client and started. You'll be happy to know it went well. The executive team was, to a man (and they were almost all men), charming and gregarious. They seemed genuinely interested and took copious notes. Truth is, at the end of the first day, I was disappointed not by my own showing, but by theirs.

Here I was, having been prepared to be challenged, called out, questioned; what I got was smiles and nods! Sure, they took part in the interactive elements and asked some good questions, but I came away from the first day with a distinct feeling of not having got enough from them. So, in a moment of derring-do and after we'd wrapped up day one, I asked the CEO if he would accept me starting day two with something of an experiment. After making sure that I wouldn't do anything he needed to check with his legal team, he gave me the go-ahead, even though I said the experiment might make his team quite angry.

I went back to my hotel room, and I wrote the greatest thing I've ever written – a 20-minute lecture on innovation *that didn't contain a single sensible sentence*. To say it was a nonsensical lecture is to misrepresent it, as it was far less sensible than that. It was every vapid article on innovation condensed into their most vapid form. It was every empty slogan about innovation distilled into something akin to Dadaist poetry. It contained not a solitary smidgen of sense. It was *wonderful*.

It started out gently, with exhortations such as 'We need to disrupt transformation and to transform disruption!' It made nonsensical claims about the power of business model innovation. About half-way through, I proudly declared the need to 'find the white spaces in the blue oceans'. It contained claims that were, frankly, close to blasphemous. And, as a kind of highlight, about 15 to 16 minutes in, it had the phrase 'So, you need to *be* the box that you think outside of!' Frankly, if you could make sense of it, it would mean that you were not so much an innovator as a zen master, fully realized and not quite on this earthly plane any longer.

I have had some training in the theatre, so when I did this lecture at the beginning of day two, it wasn't just me reading out a silly bit of innovation nonsense. On the contrary, I sold it. I talked with conviction and surety, emphasizing my nonsensical points with a great deal of impressive hand movements. I emoted and assumed dramatic power poses. In short, I did everything I could to make it seem like a proper speech. The point, obviously, was to see at what point these master innovators would realize that I was having them on, and I didn't want to make it too easy for them. Still, as I went through my list of inanities, my audience didn't react with ridicule or incredulity. They took notes.

So I gave a full 20-minute lecture of nonsense to some of the most revered innovators in the world, and not even when I asked them to be boxes they thought outside of did anyone say a peep. I, much to my surprise, got to the end of my pre-prepared nonsense and had no more nonsense to spout. A little flustered, I asked if anyone could recap what I'd been talking about so far. A very eager vice president offered to do so, only to get stumped when he couldn't make sense of his notes. I pointed out that I had only been talking utter rubbish, and that I would be surprised if his notes did make sense. I emphasized that what they'd listened to was not just nonsense, it was basically a satire of innovation talk. At this point the same vice president came back, looking not entirely unlike a sad puppy, with the comment 'But you sound just like the others'.

## Innovation lost

I tell that story not to berate the executive team of this unnamed company but to illustrate how easy it has become to be bewitched by empty innovation talk. I also use it to highlight why a culture that says it values 'innovation' isn't necessarily a culture that actually values innovation. Innovation used to mean something, but today even the smartest amongst us can become caught up in the sloganeering, the empty posturing, the verbiage. It wasn't that the executives I was lecturing were stupid. Rather, they like so many of us had become so used to superficial innovation talk that they no longer knew how to tell the parody from the reality. Just like it has become difficult to tell which Silicon Valley companies are serious startups and which are viral pranks from Comedy Central, much of today's innovation cheerleading is difficult to tell apart from satires of the same.

What this creates is not only surface effects. Sure, it is easy to laugh at stories like the one here, at overwrought PR language emanating from Palo Alto, at yet another copycat innovation book, but it is important to realize that these aren't just jokes or frivolities. For companies, all this has had both an upside and a serious downside. On the upside, the emptying out of the term innovation has meant that companies can feel much freer when it comes to marketing their activities as innovations and themselves as innovators. Companies can thus make big claims, like using 'Innovation, delivered.' as a tagline, yet be confident that they will not be called out to prove any such thing. The downside, however, is hidden in plain sight. As anything and everything becomes described as an innovation, the term has started to lose its meaning, enhancing feelings of fatigue at the face of it all.

*Describing anything and everything as an innovation is problematic on a societal level, but on the level of the firm, it can be catastrophic.*

Describing anything and everything as an innovation is problematic on a societal level, but on the level of the firm, it can be catastrophic. As innovation, as a concept, becomes emptied of meaning – by overuse, in endless meetings, by being associated with a parade of seminars and consultants – many companies have to face a situation where it no longer rallies and focuses the cognitive surplus of the firm but fatigues and bores instead. As innovation talk becomes ever more prevalent and all-encompassing, it also becomes something at best inoffensive, at worst infuriating. Despite the tremendous amount of resources most if not all organizations have for innovation, few manage to truly capitalize upon this. Many in management are caught up in the tales spun by the innovation industry and focus more on 'thinking like Elon Musk' or learning 'the three principles of world-class business model innovation' than on nurturing the ideas that emerge in their own organization – a sad state of affairs I've seen more times than I can count. Many in the organizations are fatigued by the relentless sloganeering and the parade of consultants and have all but given up. And this in an age that needs innovation more than ever.

Consider, for instance, the medtech company I recently worked with. Well positioned in their field, with a decent portfolio of steady sellers, it was being pushed by the board of directors to find new products, preferably high-margin such. The executive team attempted to do exactly this, but instead of surveying potential ideas in their organization, saw that the best way forward was an intense educational programme in new innovation methods, for primarily the executive team. A leading innovation agency was contracted to design the programme at a considerable cost. The executive team all got a large package of books to read, primarily US bestsellers in the genre. Innovation speakers were invited to give part of the programme (which was how I got involved), and a trip to California (with the mandatory visits to Google and Facebook) got booked in.

I came in half-way through the programme, gave a presentation and then settled down for some work with the group. I asked them what they wanted to achieve, why they thought they were in trouble and what they wished to achieve. The answers were... troubling. They had quickly learnt to refer to new business models and to disruptive innovation. They talked of mavericks and taking bigger risks. They discussed investing more in big data and AI. One person even talked about creating products with 'in-app purchases' – making me think of having to swipe a credit card to upgrade your pacemaker to a functional level. When I asked whether they'd been working at all with ideas such as customers not usually served by medtech companies, or creating medical technologies with impact beyond improving their bottom line, everyone looked confused. Why was I asking annoying questions when they were busy innovating? Why did I want to go deep all of a sudden?

## What is deep innovation?

Today, in both our companies and our society, much of the innovation we do and talk about is shallow innovation. We focus on the easy things, the lookalike things, the things legitimated by the media. But there is another form of innovation, one far more important, that is pushed to the back by the glitz and glamour of our current innovation hype. *Simply put, in a society in love with shallow innovation talk, deep innovation has become marginalized.*

Deep innovation might seem like a hippy-dippy term, connected with New Age notions, fake profundity and empty quotes by New Age business crossover types. This is very far from the point I wish to make. I use the term deep innovation as a counterpoint to the superficiality of much of what today goes for innovation talk, and as a badge of honour for those companies that can resist the latter. Deep innovation isn't a model, or a two-by-two matrix, or a quirky abbreviation. Instead, it is something like an ethos, a reminder that there is more to innovation than we usually see. Deep innovation is a counterpoint to overpriced smart hairbrushes with an accompanying app (yes, this exists – thanks, innovation) and to the umpteenth innovation book on how to 'think like Elon Musk'. Deep innovation is about wanting to create change rather than catering to whatever is popular right now.

Shallow innovation and deep innovation thus represent two different ways to approach and think about innovation. The former is more popular, because it emphasizes things that are easy to think about and easy to accept. It is all slogans and recognizable icons. Shallow innovation doesn't demand much more than basic obedience and the capacity to agree to some basic tenets – like the same things everyone else likes, keep things simple and don't ask any complicated questions. Shallow innovation is like a Top 10 list, inoffensive, easy to listen to and almost ensured not to have any real impact. Easily consumable, guaranteed not to be disliked by too many and, in the end, safe as milk. It shouldn't come as a surprise that corporations are all about shallow innovation, as it is everything the corporation is trained to enjoy. Safe, toothless, superficial and bland. And yet we call it innovation…

Deep innovation, on the other hand, is something else entirely. It is trying things out even if you haven't got a model for them yet. It is abrasive and challenging and hard to digest, much like every form of music that ever made an impact on the world. If shallow innovation is lift music, deep innovation is a challenging new style of expression. Deep innovation isn't as easy to like as shallow innovation, as it is more difficult to put on a poster and turn into an easily digestible recipe. Deep innovation is demanding and challenging and abrasive. In other words, tricky for corporations to deal with. And yet, it is far more important than shallow innovation could ever hope to be.

Shallow innovation is creating an app for finding the best time to go to the beach. Deep innovation is creating a way to clean plastics from the ocean. Shallow innovation is about launching yet another makeup brand. Deep innovation is about launching a service to create sustainable sewage systems in megacities. Shallow innovation is about launching one more freemium subscription service. Deep innovation is about finding a way for poor single-parent families to afford education for their children. Shallow innovation often gets the VC funding and the corporate attention. Deep innovation might save the world (see Table 1.1).

Shallow innovation cares about looks and surface, about quick bucks and novelty. Deep innovation is more engaged with

TABLE 1.1    Some elements of shallow vs deep innovation

| Shallow | Deep |
| --- | --- |
| Surface | Meaning |
| Profit | Value |
| Novelty | Impact |
| Exclusionary | Inclusive |
| Looks | Effects |
| Me-too | Unique |
| Consumption-focused | Sustainable |
| Mimicking | Ambitious |

effects and meaning, value and impact. Shallow innovation is exclusive – it's mainly for those who already have a lot, the privileged classes. Deep innovation is inclusive and tries to think about how to solve wicked problems for people who struggle. Shallow innovation loves me-too effects and likes copying business models and designs, all in order to show off that they are innovative in just the same way as everyone else. Deep innovation doesn't care about whether what it is trying to create is immediately recognizable at a swanky party in Silicon Valley, and loves truly unique approaches. Shallow innovation is a learnt behaviour, whereas deep innovation is a mindset.

Innovation is not just a thing, in other words. It can be many things and be done in many ways – some deeper than others. Still, we often talk of innovation culture as if it were a single, set, solitary thing.

## The four extremes of innovation cultures

An innovation culture isn't something that a company has or hasn't got. Every company has an innovation culture, even though it might be quite dormant and lethargic. This means that every company does engage, in some way, with novelty and new ideas. We can talk about innovation cultures on a scale of passive vs. active, but this alone is rarely enough. As I've indicated, and will highlight several times over, a corporation can be very active in the innovation sphere without this resulting in very much innovation.

It is therefore important to talk about both how companies view innovation and what kind of innovation they're going for. For the sake of simplicity, I've tended to group the innovation culture of companies by looking at whether they are interested in *impact* or *novelty*, and further whether they want to pursue something *unique* or do what their peers are doing (a *me-too* mindset). Impact here refers to innovation approaches that emphasize change, such as for instance creating a new kind of medical technology for a group that's not had access to it before. Novelty, on the other hand, emphasizes the innovation itself and whether it has new functions or other marketable aspects. Companies that attempt unique innovations are those that explore possibilities in spheres their competitors have left untouched, whereas me-too innovators are the ones who jump on a bandwagon, regardless of whether this is blockchain or cleantech.

By taking these two oppositional pairs, we get a simple two-by-two matrix, well known to anyone who has spent time with a consultant (and yes, I do realize the wild irony of this). It would look a little like the image shown in Figure 1.1.

*Shallow innovation cultures* are those that aim for novelty in their products or services, regardless of whether this has any meaningful impact or not. They follow innovation trends slavishly, so that if their peers have released something that uses augmented reality (AR) technology, they will immediately focus on the me-too goal of launching their own AR solution.

*Social innovation cultures* are cultures that do have a care for the impact of an innovation and are less occupied with the

FIGURE 1.1   Four types of innovation culture

|  | Novelty | Impact |
|---|---|---|
| Unique | Show-offs | Deep |
| Me-too | Shallow | Social |

marketability of the same, but who nevertheless are very keen to keep with the kinds of innovations that are presently popular. We might for instance think of the mass of me-too microfinancing platforms that emerged in the aftermath of Grameen Bank becoming globally recognized.

*Show-off innovation cultures* are those that are keen to do unique, big-picture things but are still more focused on the way in which their innovation is viewed than whether it can enact major change. Here we might for instance find companies that introduce highly impressive technological solutions for problems that are, at best, minor annoyances. We might for instance place quite a few of the smart home technology companies into this group.

*Deep innovation cultures* are the ones that aim for unique solutions that enact meaningful change, regardless of whether others pursue them or whether they represent the most impressive or marketable new thing. They emphasize impact and using innovation as a force of good in the world, and are unconcerned with whether their endeavours are viewed as innovations by pundits and consultants.

In practice, almost every company exhibits aspects of all four of these, and it is not impossible to e.g. find one part of the corporation being very much a show-off innovation culture whereas another is a deep one. Looking for instance to two of the more popular examples in the innovation literature, Apple and Tesla, we can see this specific mixture in both. The 'insane mode' in Tesla cars[8] is for instance a classic show-off, whereas the strive towards all-electric transport is both impactful and unique. In a similar vein, Apple has done some very deep innovation with how they approach making digital tools approachable for all, whereas the updating cycles of the iPhone have often been criticized as veering towards show-offs, even shallow innovation.[9]

Thus your task is to a) understand the current innovation culture in your company, and b) see whether it would be possible to make your innovation culture at least a little bit deeper. The trouble is, this doesn't come naturally. Quite the contrary. There isn't just 'innovation'. There are many forms of innovation, and not all are as deserving of our praise. Just like there are good policies and bad ones, or real news and fake news, there are serious, impactful innovations and superficial, silly ones. The problem? Today, shallow innovation has far better marketing and PR. In fact, there's an entire industry built up around boosting shallow innovation.

## The innovation industry

Innovation, particularly shallow innovation, didn't get to be the be-all and end-all of concept all on its own. On the contrary, one of the most interesting things about the modern preoccupation with innovation is the exceptional apparatus that exists only to boost the concept and create a never-ending torrent of hype around it. Innovation, today, is an industry all of its own, one that consists of numerous actors, and shallow innovation is their product. There are the innovation consultants whose income is dependent on convincing companies they need help in order to be innovative. There are the innovation pundits whose stock in trade are easy truths about innovation. Then there are the innovation books, the products of the aforementioned groups.

It should come as no surprise that different aspects of this industry feed into and support one another. Shallow innovation courses assign shallow innovation books, innovation conferences need innovation pundits, and the innovation networks require innovation consultants to write a seemingly endless stream of content for various online outlets. The fact that much of what happens in all of this is the rehashing of the same few ideas over and over again doesn't really bother anyone. In fact, shallow, recognizable and easy to digest are part and parcel of what the industry is about! Whilst its agents would bristle and protest against it as a description of what they do, the innovation industry is really less about boosting the new and more about creating a sense of security. The endless repetition of a few core examples – Apple, Google, Amazon and Tesla – makes innovation sound well known and well understood and ensures that audiences are never exposed to anything too radical or out there. Easily recognizable models and thinkers complete the picture, and as innovation authors mostly quote other innovation authors, an almost perfect filter bubble of innovation is established.

What this creates is a key arena for discussions about innovation that is both remarkably un-innovative and that also turns innovation into something quite dull. Whilst the first innovation book may well energize a company, the tenth is markedly less inspiring, and the hundredth may well infuriate – particularly as the repetition of the same basic ideas becomes quite grating. Simply put, the industrialization of innovation thinking, leading to an abundance of shallow innovation talk, becomes the very thing that creates innovation fatigue.

## Innovation commodified

At play here is a significant transformation in how we view innovation. This used to be seen as an event, a major shift, something that happened when the right people got together to change the world. Today, thanks to the innovation industry, it is increasingly seen as a commodity, something you can buy. No-one would of course say this out loud, but the key logic of the innovation industry is precisely this – commodifying innovation.

Here, innovation becomes something you pick up if you read the right books, go to the right conferences and use the right methods, taught on the right courses. Here, innovation is something you buy from an innovation consultancy. Today, you can take courses that claim to make you a certified 'Innovation Master' and progress on to become a certified 'Innovation Leader' – for a fee, naturally. Companies also go to great lengths to sell themselves as innovators, and in doing so they take part in the great mill that is the innovation industry. Relentless innovation PR and an unending stream of innovation articles attempt to hammer home the message that we too do innovation, often so that the less innovative a company is, the more it attempts to churn out reports and the like to at least look the part.

*What happens when employees feel that managers are more interested in the upcoming innovation report than in their actual ideas?*

But what happens in organizations where innovation more and more becomes a word affixed to posters, part of cheery slogans screen printed on the t-shirts distributed at the yearly innovation event?

What happens when employees feel that managers are more interested in the upcoming innovation report than in their actual ideas? What happens when innovation becomes something you take courses in, not something you do at work? It becomes, in a word, shallow. It becomes all surface effects, and in the long run, this drains us. Which is unfortunate, for what we need is more energy to innovate, more imagination, not less of it. How can this conundrum be solved?

## The haves and have-nots of the imagination economy

The role of ideas, creativity, innovation and imagination as key drivers in every economic model, on every level, is so well established that it doesn't need reiteration – despite the popularity of such. In short, we know that companies, particularly in situations defined by intense competition and fast-changing environments (as if there would be any others, these days...), need to use their imagination, develop ideas and create innovations. We know it, the companies know it, their CEOs know it, even the politicians know it. Were we somehow to forget, we can always count upon the innovation industry to remind us, over and over again.

This universal agreement when it comes to the importance and value of creativity and innovation hasn't translated into all companies becoming hotbeds of ideas and imagination, however. In fact, as most of us would probably attest to, there are a lot more companies that proclaim to have innovation as a core value than there are companies that actually live that ideal. Looking to the data, we can see that innovation fatigue has had very tangible effects. Whilst recognizing the importance of creativity, many companies are today increasingly worried about their capacity to actually generate good ideas and execute the same. A frequently repeated statistic from research conducted by McKinsey[10] states that a whopping 94 per cent of CEOs are displeased with how well their companies innovate.

For me, this is a fascinating conundrum. Organizations know they have to become more innovative, and they seem to talk of little else. Massive resources are invested in research and development, not to mention in an unending parade of workshops, seminars, consultants and glitzy conferences. Yet, at the same time, in the very same organizations, there is a palpable sense of dread and worry regarding these issues, as well as noticeable fatigue. Which has led me to a critical question, one that has been niggling at me for some time. What if all this talk about innovation isn't the solution, but the problem?

Our contemporary innovation talk *is* shallow, and that *is* a problem. It is not unsolvable, but it is serious. We need a new conversation about innovation, one that breaks with the innovation industry and with the superficial hailing of a limited set of examples. A conversation that builds stronger cultures and energizes people rather than creates exhaustion. A change in approach that can capture the enormous potential that still exists in most if not all companies, the massive amount of cognitive surplus that we today waste and squander.

## Our cognitive surplus

When I give keynotes on creativity and innovation, I often return to the same key insight. I may sound quite negative when it comes to the innovation capacity of contemporary companies, but this is only part of the picture. In fact, I also see that whilst we have made innovation shallow, the capacity for deep innovation is still there – and how! I have by now worked with hundreds of companies, in various guises. In each and every one of them, I've taken some time to chat with people in the organization, preferably a few steps down from the C-suite, both in groups and one on one. These talks, these explorations of the companies that claim they struggle with ideas, has led me to a realization: it's simply not true that they lack ideas. No organization lacks ideas. Not really, *not a single one*. No, not the one you work in either...

On the contrary, in each and every one of the companies I've worked with, it has taken me at most minutes, sometimes just seconds, to discover new ideas. Give me an hour, and I can find dozens. Give me a day, and it might be 100. And it didn't matter if the company was a hip and on trend IT company or a government agency. I found ideas in companies making welding equipment and in companies focused on elderly care. In fact, the more traditional a company called itself, the more likely it was to have a plethora of ideas bubbling in the culture, even though this bubbling could at times be quite repressed and hidden away. *There is not now, nor has there ever been, an organization that lacks ideas.*

*There is not now, nor has there ever been, an organization that lacks ideas.*

Instead, each company I've worked with, and this includes companies that had an extremely traditional reputation and those that were being slaughtered by the competition, has been positively brimming over with ideas. Ideas are simply not the problem. Ideas are cheap. Ideas can be generated in bulk, at speed. Ideas are important, but they are also plentiful. The challenge is: do we know how to use them? Or, to put this in a slightly different manner: do we even know the innovation resources we have?

In 2010, the American media theorist Clay Shirky wrote a book by the name *Cognitive Surplus: Creativity and generosity in a connected age*. In this, he argued that the new tools of connection and collaboration that the internet spawned could be understood as engines for capturing society's 'cognitive surplus', i.e. the power of human minds that might otherwise be idle. When people, rather than sitting in front of the TV, start creating fan art, editing Wikipedia and collaborate on projects both whimsical and important, this meant that the cognitive surplus was being directed into more active and more valuable pursuits. It is a delightful, if slightly romantic idea, and it points to a very important observation regarding innovation – all organizations have far more innovation potential than we give them credit for.[11]

Today, in just about every company the world over, there is an army of highly educated people, all equipped with computing technology that would have seemed inconceivable 25 years ago and nigh on magical 50 years ago. They all carry supercomputers in their pockets (or handbags), incredible devices that can access much or even most information in the world at the click of an icon. It is not unlikely that they have received at least basic training in creativity and innovation, and many of them have explored far more complex topics, such as innovation management tools or models of business model innovation. Taken together, even a small company's innovation resources amount to something akin to a super-intelligence, one with enough ideas and cognitive cycles to drive an entire economy.

Yet what does the average company do with this goldmine of ideas and innovation potential? Well, most companies seem content to keep them in their cubicles or in meetings, with occasional outings during which they will be exhorted to 'think outside the box' (this most vile of clichéd expressions). The fact is that for most managers, the employees you have right now are the cognitive surplus of the company, and they're being squandered. In fact, they might not even know what they're supposed to do any more, and shallow innovation is to blame.

## Innovation rich

This challenge is what this book is about. We live in a world with great challenges and wicked problems, and innovation is one of the best weapons we have in this fight. On the other hand we live in a world with shallow innovation talk and an increasing sense that there's something amiss with innovation. I see, and work with, companies with tremendous resources, a plethora of talent, a capacity to truly make a dent in the universe, and I see them beset by fatigue, stress and confusion. As noted Silicon Valley whiz kid Jeff Hammerbacher put it, 'The best minds of my generation are thinking about how to make people click ads. That sucks'.[12] At some point, innovation – in society and in organizations – stopped being about the big things.

At the same time, innovation amassed more potential than ever before. We've already mentioned the tremendous amount of cognitive surplus that every organization, not to mention society as a whole, has. But that's not all. Yes, we have more knowledge than ever before and better technologies, but we also have more money to spend on innovation than we've ever had. It isn't easy to get a perfect figure for how much we spend on innovation globally, but we can get an approximation of minimum expenditure. Several leading research organizations, amongst them the OECD, have estimated corporate expenditure on R&D, which is considered to be at the core of innovation expense. To this figure, we need to add various other expenditures – government-supported research, venture capital outlays on innovative companies, support for innovations in the non-profit sector, even investments in things like business model innovation. Different entities have suggested different equations for evaluating total expenditure, but we can use the one suggested by the OECD as a base figure that is almost certainly going to be too low. They suggest that total expenditure on innovation can be estimated by taking R&D expenditure and adding on 50 to 100 per cent to reach a final figure.

Global R&D expenditure has, since the 2010s, hovered around US $2 trillion.[13] That is US $2,000 billion, or US $2 million million. If we use the lowest estimate of the OECD to obtain a total figure, that would mean adding another US $1 trillion to this, reaching US $3 trillion, or US $3,000,000,000,000.

To put this into perspective, you might consider the gross domestic product of all the Nordic countries, that is Sweden, Denmark, Norway, Finland and Iceland (with Greenland and the Faroe Islands thrown in to boot). Whilst small, these are all considered rich countries and fairly advanced. Their total GDPs add up to approximately US $1.5 trillion. In other words, we spend twice the total economy of the Nordic countries every year on innovation.

In fact, I would argue that this figure is a low estimate. Even the OECD allows for the fact that it might be a full US $1 trillion higher, amounting to about the GDP of Germany. Personally, I think the OECD's estimate for total innovation expenditure is lowballing it, and that the full figure might be as high as US $5 trillion, but who's counting, and what's a trillion between friends? No lack of resources, in other words. No lack of enthusiasm. No lack of innovation talk; quite the contrary. Definitely no lack of innovation books or consultants. No lack of talent. No lack of ideas. Still, considering these inputs, questions need to be asked about the output. What, really, is our *ROII* (Return On Innovation Investment), and what can we do to improve it?

## Big idea famine

Succinctly put, what shallow innovation has done is that it has skewed our view on innovation. On a societal level, this means that both resources and attention have tended to go more to companies that live up to the hype of the innovation industry, rather than to solving vexing problems. As famed venture capitalist Ross Baird writes in his insightful book *The Innovation Blind Spot: Why we back the wrong ideas – and what to do about it,*[14] the way in which we for instance have iconized Silicon Valley has in fact damaged innovation. The limited, shallow view on innovation that is still looking for the next Steve Jobs, and looking predominantly amongst bright, white techies from 'the right schools', in fact misses out on many of the best and most impactful ideas. As governments and funding agencies become dazzled by the astronomic valuations of unicorn start-ups, deep innovation that comes from less iconized backgrounds and focuses on more mundane and fundamental issues often becomes marginalized.

Nicholas Negroponte, founder of the MIT Media Lab, has talked about a 'big idea famine',[15] stating that our age is self-congratulatory regarding innovation whilst missing out on the opportunity to do something about long-term problems. He calls out Apple, perennial favourite of the innovation pundits, for siphoning off ideas from basic research and then locking this up in their own organization and their own walled gardens. Sharing none of their internal research (even forbidding their researchers to go to scientific conferences) and pouring money into ever-better smartphone cameras whilst ignoring basic research into computing and technology, Apple might in Negroponte's telling be one of innovation's prime enemies. Or consider the arguments regarding 'solutionism', as these have been put forward by the noted critical thinker Evgeny Morozov. Pointing to the technological optimism from the tech industry (and promulgated by the innovation pundits), he notes that the manner in which both problems and solutions are cast in fact limits the alternatives we have and bind us closer to a few corporations – for our own good, obviously. With a limited number of companies (sometimes we refer to FAANG – Facebook, Apple, Amazon, Netflix and Google – as something akin to a mythical monster) becoming more and more dominant, Morozov asks whether we are just to trust these to behave altruistically when they are incentivized to be everything but.[16]

In a similar vein, Erixon and Weigel have in the title of their book referred to *The Innovation Illusion: How so little is created by so many working so hard*,[17] stating that current corporate practices, not to mention government policies, are decreasing economic dynamism and in effect choking corporate innovation.

With more and more resources bound up in projects that are either incremental, serve to solve non-essential problems (you can today preorder the FoldiMate, a washing-machine-sized product that folds your laundry – if you insert it correctly, one piece at a time), or simply follow whatever the innovation industry has deigned to be the technology flavour of the season (at the time of writing, blockchain and anything with a remote connection to robots). They do not refer to shallow innovation, but their view is very much in line with the notion that there is a fundamental superficiality in how corporations and countries view the same.

The scary fact is that whilst we believe ourselves to be living in an age of innovation, historical data shows a very different picture. Robert J. Gordon's magisterial *The Rise and Fall of American Growth*[18] showed in an arresting manner how dynamic our economies were in the period from 1920 to 1970, bolstered by the age of great inventions (railroads, electricity, indoor plumbing) that preceded it. Today, we might see decreasing extreme poverty, but also a collapsing middle class and a continuous downward trend for overall productivity. And this in an age when we invest more than ever in innovation! Whilst the innovation industry is busy hailing the latest iteration of the sharing economy, many companies see their ROII suffering. More and more resources put into innovation beget less and less impressive results. In computer engineering people used to talk of Moore's Law, which stated that every two years we could double the number of transistors that could fit onto an integrated circuit. For a long time this held true, and computers became ever faster and more amazing. This law was often hailed by the innovation industry as proof positive of innovation's endless progress, and it was heavily hinted at that everything else could develop apace to computers, thanks to the magic of 'digitalization'. The only trouble? Moore's Law no longer holds, even in computing. In many other areas, first in the pharmaceutical industry but now in more and more industries, we're instead seeing Eroom's Law. Rather than predicting endless progress, this suggests a rapid deceleration. For every two years, you need to invest twice as much in innovation *to stay where you were*. Like the Red Queen says in *Alice in Wonderland*, 'My dear, here we must run as fast as we can, just to stay in place. And if you wish to go anywhere you must run twice as fast as that'.

## The research behind this book, or the companies fighting famine and fatigue

Now, I am the last person to suggest that all is lost, and there are companies who've shown a remarkable skill in running twice as fast as they can. There are companies who have managed to beat innovation fatigue and Eroom's Law, who've managed to capture their innate cognitive surplus and ignore the siren calls of shallow innovation. These are the companies that are attempting deep innovation, and this book is about how to build an innovation culture that can do just that. Companies that are able to combat what Ed Catmull, of Pixar fame, has referred to as 'the fragility of ideas'.[19] Companies that can take the riches of our resource and direct them towards solving wicked, meaningful problems.

This book is the product of a decade-long fascination with the field of corporate innovation and how it is squandered. I have, since the early 2000s, in one way or another, worked with hundreds of companies, in almost every industry imaginable. I have worked with them as an academic, interviewing people and poring through archives. I have worked with them as a strategic adviser, listening to CEOs and sitting in on board meetings. Over time, I started realizing just how much innovation was wasted in companies and just how much could be attributed to their culture. I saw some companies in the grips of shallow innovation miss wonderful ideas simply because they did not fit with the narrative of the latest business book, and others who managed to engage every single person in their organization to push for deep innovation. This book is the result of these travels between the shallows and the deep blue sea.

What follows will be an exploration of the companies and the cultures that can go beyond the precepts of the innovation industry. We will explore a chemical company that used a lack of respect and Excel to kill their employees' desire to innovate, and another that managed to do the opposite with a simple little pill. We will look to why faster isn't always better when it comes to innovation, and how a small company found new thinking and rapid growth simply by raising their level of innovation ambition. We will look to the major technology company that managed to re-energize its culture simply by banning the word 'innovation'. We will look to how easy it is to be lured by shallow innovation and innovation punditry, and what is needed to truly go deep with innovation.

Most important of all, I will in this book try to argue for two things:

One, if we can't look critically on innovation and innovation talk, we can't develop next-level innovation thinking. To solve a problem you must understand the problem, and today we talk far too little about the problems inherent in superficial innovation thinking.

Two, the thing missing from most innovation cultures isn't one more model or one more strategic theory, but rather something far more fundamental. It is making innovation into something meaningful for people. The core elements of healthy innovation cultures are not a tolerance for risk and a propensity for brainstorming but instead deeper values like respect (for people and ideas), reciprocity and a generosity of spirit, responsibility and the courage to be vulnerable, and a genuine reflection about what it all means.

This is a book on innovation, and with the plethora of such out there, one might ask why anyone would wish to write another. I wanted to write this not to repeat the same old truisms but to say a number of things about innovation that today have been marginalized by the innovation industry. I wanted to write something that celebrates those who still want to go deep in an increasingly shallow age.

## The rest of this book

The book will continue in the following manner:

In Chapter 2, we will look to *how ideas die in contemporary organizations*. We can't start saving innovation, nor develop ideas towards something deeper and more meaningful, until we understand what it is in our culture(s) that hinders ideas from flourishing.

In Chapter 3, the art and science of *crafting innovation cultures* will be explored. Looking to how psychological safety, reciprocity and reflection can be used to build cultures where people wish to voice their ideas and make innovation meaningful, we will build a base for an organization for deep innovation.

In Chapter 4, we turn our attention to *imagination and play*, not as childish frivolities but as mission-critical aspects of real innovation, the kind that dares question the *status quo* and push innovation towards something greater – even something previously unimaginable.

In Chapter 5, we look to *the critical dimension of diversity*. No organization can innovate deeply without a diverse stock of ideas and perspectives, and this chapter discusses the complexities of instilling deep diversity in the innovative organization.

In Chapter 6, the issues are *purpose, courage and ambition*. A safe and nurturing culture is necessary for deep innovation, but this needs to be coupled with a desire to go beyond the showy part of innovation and to make it meaningful.

In Chapter 7, last but certainly not least, the topic is *the many speeds of innovation*. A central part of how innovation is lost in corporations is a lack of understanding of why deep innovation takes its time, why we need fast experiments and how we can craft a culture that can encompass the differing tempos of innovation.

The book ends with Chapter 8, which deals with how we can *pull all this together*. You don't just craft or build an innovation culture, you nurture it day by day. Innovation and culture are both things that are never finished and finalized but living, breathing things that need constant support so as to not become shallow and superficial anew.

# CHAPTER TWO

# Of yawns and broken windows

*How ideas die in the modern corporation*

'*Never expect someone to understand change when their livelihood depends on not understanding it.*' UPTON SINCLAIR

## Human ingenuity in an age of AI

We are often told that the coming age of competition will be all about data and artificial intelligence (AI). In this age, we're told, the valuable employees aren't the creatives, but data analysts of various assignations, able to tweak the all-important algorithms of the smart company. Further than this, some claim that the company of the future won't be defined by human thinking at all, but by ever-improving algorithms, machine learning and, sooner or later, AIs.

Whilst data will no doubt be important, and whilst digitalization (a sloppy term, but one that will have to do) will drive a lot of development, the notion that human ingenuity would be muscled out by increasingly intelligent machines is deeply flawed. Yes, there might come a time in which machines acquire imagination, creativity and the skills required for radical innovation, but even for a technological optimist such as myself, these are many, many decades away. Whilst our great-great-great-grandchildren may enjoy lives of endless leisure, we who are here now still need to create competitive advantage in the old-fashioned way – through human ingenuity. The fact is, this will be valuable long after things such as machine learning have become an everyday occurrence in corporations.

The reason for this is quite simple. *Data-driven improvement, whilst not unimportant, is not the same as innovation.* Yes, data is important. Yes, machine learning will bring us great things. But these are things that will supercharge business as usual, hone the processes we already know and improve the things we already know. Real innovation, the kind that looks beyond what we do and know now, will for the foreseeable future – and quite possibly far beyond that – be founded on the quirky capacity of human beings to think in entirely novel ways. No algorithm would have been able to consider starting a hotel business without owning any hotels. No form of machine learning would have been able to make the leap from a service-based business such as airlines to a no-service business such as low-cost airlines. Such leaps, which often seem irrational and illogical, are what humans are great at – and as we do not even know exactly how humans manage to make such leaps, we cannot easily expect that we can teach it to machines. Particularly ones that are defined by logic and reason.

## The new productivity

What this means is that companies that wish to secure a competitive advantage can't trust digitalization any more than they can rely on 'best practice'. The latter, which I often refer to as 'sh-t that used to work', is built on historical reason. The former draws on creating efficiencies around things we already know. Only creativity, imagination and ingenuity can consistently create difficult-to-copy advantages, yet, as I've already indicated, most organizations treat these things in a manner that produces fatigue and stress rather than workable solutions; something Hollister and Watkins have referred to as 'initiative overload'.[1]

*What the company that desires success needs to do is twofold: defeat innovation fatigue and build creative cultures.* Defeating innovation fatigue and building creative cultures are steps that can capture and benefit from the cognitive surplus that already exists in an organization, and neither step can be achieved by mindlessly repeating mantras about innovation or digitalization. In fact, the latter may be counter-productive as well, because it is stuck in an old way of thinking about productivity.

*What the company that desires success needs to do is twofold: defeat innovation fatigue and build creative cultures.*

In the old system, productivity was all about getting people to work with machines, or like machines. Efficiency was the order of the day, and it was measured in throughput. More and faster meant better. Faster processes, more data points, a greater intensity of action. Machine learning fits perfectly into this mindset, a sci-fi update to assembly lines and Fordist mass production. Earlier, employees had to do busywork by hand, whilst in the bright new world of work, an AI can engage in infinite amounts of busywork. Hooray for productivity!

The real new productivity is something else entirely. In this, productivity is measured by how well an organization manages to capture cognitive surplus. Rather than seeing just how efficiently it can replicate the systems of yesteryear, the successes of this new era are the ones that track just how many novel ideas their organization can create, tend to, nurture, bring to fruition. We have seen this transformation before. In the Soviet Union, some factories realized that no-one cared if they produced something sensible or not, as long as their output was deemed impressive. So a shoe-making factory might eschew making shoes for the left foot, as making only right-foot shoes created more impressive results. A factory making rebar steel couldn't care less if the rebar was usable, as long as they made lots of it.[2] This is machine learning, this is AI. Over time, however, this resulted in an economic system with seemingly impressive efficiencies that created nothing that people actually wanted or needed.

In our age, we can see something similar. We have companies pumping out endless iterations of 'innovative' new toys, as well as corporations that claim innovation is one of their core values, whilst ignoring all inputs that do not come from the very top of the organization. We have venture capital streaming to me-too products and companies flocking to copy the latest innovation snake oil. The real successes of tomorrow will come from something else. It will come from companies that refuse this kind of fake efficiency and focus instead on building the kinds of cultures where challenging current efficiencies and best practices are seen as the greatest productivity of all. It will come from companies ready to reject reductionist models of innovation and who instead embrace inclusivity, respect and diversity. It will come from companies prepared to reject shallow innovation. But in order to do this, they need to become better at connecting with ideas and the deep insights that exist within their cognitive surplus. Doing this, again, requires understanding the life cycle of ideas and, above all, how ideas die.

## On inhospitable contexts

Few people think it's a great idea to establish a vineyard in Siberia. Fewer still try to establish a major flower farming operation in Saudi Arabia. Almost no-one thinks that Alaska is a great place to create a banana empire. Fewer still think that what creativity needs is a great big bureaucracy. Granted, there may be a few brave souls who have tried out one or more of these endeavours, even if I've never heard of one. If they have, and succeeded to boot, they deserve our admiration, but the reason very few have is that ideas are context-dependent.

This should come as no surprise to anyone who has ever attempted to present an idea in a context obviously hostile to the same, nor to anyone who has experienced the heady joy of having an idea generously, immediately and excitedly accepted because it fitted in with the context in which it was proposed. This notwithstanding, we often talk of innovation as if it were a power that can win over even the most inhospitable of contexts and that the best idea will always win. Both are highly problematic assumptions.

In practice, what we often see in organizations is that great ideas are often first ignored, then actively opposed, after which starts a process of euthanasia for the few ideas that simply will not die. Consider, for example, the story of Gary Starkweather. A laser specialist working at Xerox's first research centre, he had the first (conceptually complete) idea for the laser printer. Now, you would think it fortuitous that this idea came to a laser specialist in a research centre for a world-leading office-equipment company and that it would be received with great interest. This would be a mistake. He presented the idea to his boss, who immediately declared that it was too expensive, too complicated and just dumb. After working on the idea in secret, Starkweather asked to be transferred to another research centre, the legendary Xerox PARC. Yes, that place. The place where Steve Jobs got the idea for the Macintosh and without which we might have neither personal computers nor the internet. In other words, one of the most iconic places in innovation history, fetishized as one of the most hospitable contexts for ideas ever.

At Xerox PARC, he got to pursue his idea of a laser printer, but not without resistance. Whilst the centre experimented with printing technologies, many in management considered this a mistake – particularly when it came to the foolish idea of a laser printer. Of the three groups working on printing, one had a budget for 50 people, the other only enough for 20. The 'group' working on laser printing had two. Yes, two. Even after there had been an internal competition, which the laser printer technology easily won, management was not won over. The idea survived, but only just.[3]

This might seem like a very pessimistic message. If ideas have to struggle to survive, even in the mythical labs of Xerox PARC, what chance is there for them in the average corporation? Still, I think the lesson is actually the opposite. There is no magical place for ideas, and even the smartest organizations occasionally fumble. Ideas can die almost anywhere, no matter how storied the organization, so it is up to us to understand how to create a culture where ideas and innovation have a chance, where even a fledgling idea can be nurtured into something great. But to do that, we need to get better at understanding ideas. And not of how they're born, as most books on innovation focus on, but how they die.

## The lonesome death of most ideas

We greatly misunderstand the death of ideas, particularly in organizations. There is a highly problematic assumption in much of what is said about how organizations hinder ideas and creativity, and this is that it primarily happens in an overt and explicit manner. When we talk of organizations, we often populate our stories of them with a special breed of people, 'Those Who Don't Get It'. We then talk of these people as if they walk around in organizations and actively bash ideas with great violence and alacrity. It's the accountant that scoffs at our idea,

*For the best idea-killing device, look no further than the humble and ever-present yawn.*

the colleagues that sabotage us, the boss who says 'No, I'm sorry, but definitely not'. This notion that most ideas are actively killed, in a visible and overt manner, is a huge misunderstanding. It is far more common that creativity is quashed in a passive, quiet way, one where the people doing the killing don't even realize they're doing it. Most ideas die from neglect and a lack of care, not overt opposition and criticism. *For the best idea-killing device, look no further than the humble and ever-present yawn.*

Imagine a meeting in almost any organization you can think of. In this little tableau, we can see how most ideas in organizations really die. It goes a little like this:

'Hey, listen; I have an idea!'

'...'

'Do you want to hear it?'

'Um. Yeeaah... Is there any coffee?'

'I think so, check the pot. So do you want to hear my idea?'

'I guess... OK, what the hell.'

'What if, instead of using process A, we'd build a new system, one where customers could run the complaints-handling process themselves?'

'(Yaawwwn) Uh... I... Well. You know. It'd need a line in the budget.'

'Don't you like my idea?'

'I guess. I'll think about it. We're out of coffee, by the way.'

Nothing in this little scenario points to a distinct 'No' or a 'Your idea is stupid and a waste of time'. It doesn't contain direct criticism, neither does it state that the idea is worthless. In fact, if you look at it without understanding social codes, it even looks a little supportive. The person listening to the idea gives several assurances, a vaguely positive answer and even promises to think about the idea. That is, unless you understand how people and thus organizations work.

If you've ever worked in or worked with an organization, you can say a number of things about this little vignette – which, although not a verbatim depiction of a conversation, is an honest-to-God retelling of a scene I've seen not only in one company but in a number of them. You'll also know that the silence that follows when somebody proclaims they have an idea is both uncomfortable and all too common. This is, in a very fundamental way, how ideas die. Not by being criticized to death, not by being viciously attacked. No, the usual way ideas die is in silence. Unloved, uncared for, utterly alone and ignored. And we are all complicit.

## When you're the Sphinx

Nobody wants to hear that they are one of the enemies of creativity in an organization. On the contrary, even the suggestion that they might be can enrage people. Take for instance the highly passive-aggressive COO of a telecom company I once worked with. He was famously taciturn and often listened to pitches for new products or processes in a manner where his stony visage and almost complete lack of reactions ensured that only the very bravest in the organization pitched something to him more than once. In interviews people talked of him as almost a mythological being, a Cerberus that few managed to get beyond. In meetings, I'd observed this live as people came in with a clear spring in their step, delighted to present a new notion, only to turn ashen and lose their positive demeanour as they realized that the COO was present.

As an exit interview of sorts I then sat down with the COO and broached the subject with him. I said that the interviews and my observations indicated that one of the things that was hindering innovation in the company was his behaviour, more specifically the way in which his body language and lack of response signalled a negative attitude towards new ideas. He was not happy to hear this. In fact, he got quite angry. He suggested that rather than accusing him, people in the organization should focus on bucking up their ideas and stated that he was more than willing to support good ideas. Also, he said, he made it a point never to criticize ideas the first time he heard them.

Interestingly, he was right about this last point. He never did, and in his mind it meant that he hadn't quashed any ideas. What he failed to notice was that inaction can be an action as well. People in the organization weren't reacting to his active killing of ideas, as they rarely if ever got that far. Instead they were reacting to his utter lack of engagement. He listened, sure, but like a Sphinx – which one of my interviewees memorably called him. Unmoved, unsmiling, unresponsive – when he wasn't yawning, which he quite often did. I told this to him and pointed out that such behaviours, such *micro-behaviours*, could be just as impactful as an overt 'No'. At which point he bristled and confidently stated, 'But I'm never unresponsive!'

Very few of us actually understand our own micro-behaviours, those hundreds of little things that affect people around us.[4] Even people who've been married for decades can be unaware of how their little sideways glances can be interpreted by their life partners (a fact that has kept couple's counsellors in business for close to a century). We all, at times, adopt demeanours that signal to the world around us that we're not interested, not really engaging. The reasons for this can be manifold, and we will get back to these reasons, but the important thing to notice here is that we've all sat in meetings and looked utterly bored and uninterested. We may not have intended to, but we've all been the Sphinx at one point or another.

The interesting thing here is that this little thing, this micro-behaviour of adopting a stony, unsmiling exterior, can have effects far beyond what the person displaying it has intended. It, together with other micro-behaviours, can be important building blocks in creating an inhospitable context for ideas and creativity.

## Broken windows theory

What makes a community fail? Why do some neighbourhoods flourish whilst others fall into disarray? And why do some organizations, despite their best intentions, sink into torpor, not unlike a dinosaur in a tar pit? We often start looking for one of two things when trying to answer such questions. Either we look for a villain, somebody who personally caused this, or we look for a major crisis. In the former case, we are happy to blame a CEO or a President, a foreman or a mayor, and unequivocally state that they are the root of the problem. In the latter case, we look for something like drugs, or the closing of a factory, or the limitless arrogance of techies, anything that makes it clear that one specific major factor was the cause of collapse. Very few blame broken windows. But some do, and they may have a point.

In criminology, the term is well known. In 1982, in an article in *The Atlantic* entitled 'Broken Windows: The Police and Neighborhood Safety', the social scientists James Q. Wilson and George L. Kelling suggested that social disorder was far more dependent on minor shifts than previously thought. Citing work by Philip Zimbardo, they suggested that even a small sign that bad behaviour was acceptable could radically shift the way a community behaved. Their summation of Zimbardo's experiment is worth quoting at length:

> Philip Zimbardo, a Stanford psychologist, reported in 1969 on some experiments testing the broken-window theory. He arranged to have an automobile without license plates parked with its hood up on a street in the Bronx and a comparable automobile on a street in Palo Alto, California. The car in the Bronx was attacked by 'vandals' within ten minutes of its 'abandonment'. The first to arrive were a family – father, mother, and young son – who removed the radiator and battery. Within twenty-four hours, virtually everything of value had been removed. Then random

destruction began – windows were smashed, parts torn off, upholstery ripped. Children began to use the car as a playground. Most of the adult 'vandals' were well-dressed, apparently clean-cut whites. The car in Palo Alto sat untouched for more than a week. Then Zimbardo smashed part of it with a sledgehammer. Soon, passersby were joining in. Within a few hours, the car had been turned upside down and utterly destroyed. Again, the 'vandals' appeared to be primarily respectable whites.[5]

The central story here is not that Bronx is a bad area, or that Palo Alto is a nice one. The car in the Bronx was designed to show that no-one cared about it – the lack of licence plates being a dead giveaway. The parked car in Palo Alto had all the trappings that someone did care for it, until it didn't. The moment Zimbardo 'broke the window' of the car, this acted as a signal to the surrounding community that it was free game. What Wilson and Kelling inferred out of this, as well as out of their own research into neighbourhoods and communities, was that small signs of a lack of care can have oversize effects, something later adopted in e.g. zero tolerance policing.

There is a clear lesson here for companies. Yes, every company states that they value creativity and innovation. No company, anywhere, has ever said they dislike new ideas. Most companies spend a fortune on innovation initiatives and various projects designed to generate and capture ideas. What they often fail to notice is the many, many broken windows that these can contain.

## How to kill innovation culture with an idea competition, part 1

Some years ago I worked with a major corporation in the chemical industry. Whilst not a BASF or a similar top five company in the industry, they were a large global player, well-known in their segment. Unfortunately, their segment was one of low-margin bulk chemicals and strongly affected by globalization. In short, the company was hanging on and still profitable, but only barely. The executive team had realized the challenge this posed and understood that they needed to enhance their innovation capabilities, as well as be on the lookout for new, radical ideas. I had worked a little with them in trying to scope this, but I also felt that some of their stated enthusiasm was blunted by their dislike of doing anything particularly novel and new. As part of their process, the executive team had come across the brainstorm that an internal ideas competition would be well aligned with their new innovation strategy. I had cautioned against this, as I know just how difficult it is to execute such competitions well, and, as I suspected, the visibility of it could overtake more important engagements. The team was adamant, however, and I did what I could to help them design the competition for maximum impact.

In the beginning it looked like the competition was a huge success. It ended up generating more than 700 ideas, and as the demands on the ideas when it came to documentation and development were fairly stringent, this was a great result. Most of the ideas were considered and feasible, and the executive team (supplanted with other trusted members of the organization) had to work hard to whittle their shortlist down to six. These six were to be presented at a finale later in the year.

Some weeks before this finale I visited one of the European offices of the company. As it so happens, by the lifts I bumped into a man I'd met on a few occasions before. We got chatting, and he asked me what I was doing in the company. I mentioned that I'd been doing a little work on the idea competition, whereupon he stated 'Ah, yes. That. I learnt a lot from that'. Delighted to hear this I asked what he had learnt from it, and he answered, 'Well, I learned never to share an idea with this company again!' Taken aback by this somewhat unusual reaction on an idea competition I asked why that was, and he told me what had happened.

He had at first been excited by the idea competition and decided to take part. Being an experienced chemical engineer, he had several things he'd been mulling, and he quickly wrote up brief reports on two of these. Thrilled by how quickly he'd managed this, he then worked in the evenings and at weekends to develop his first two and documenting a further three ideas, ending up submitting five ideas in all. He stated that he didn't really expect any of these to be shortlisted, as the company had hired quite a few young and ambitious people as of late, but still felt thrilled about getting to take part. The problem, he said, was not that he hadn't been shortlisted (he hadn't) but what he realized once this was communicated. He had gone to his laptop one day, only to notice an email with the subject line 'Results of the idea competition'. Opening this, he read the following email, quoted here in full:

'Thank you for taking part in the idea competition. We got many excellent submissions, could only shortlist a few, and unfortunately your idea was not among them'.

That's it. No feedback, no signature, nothing more. At this point of the story I express my shock and dismay at the brevity of the email and how horrified I was over it not even being signed. To which he said, 'Oh, that's not the problem. We're a very technical culture, we don't go for all that flowery stuff. If it wasn't shortlisted, it wasn't shortlisted. And I don't need a signature! I can see from the email program who sent it'. At this point I am thoroughly confused and end up just asking what the problem then might have been? 'I didn't just get one email. I got five identical ones. And at that point I realized they didn't care about me at all. What I considered ideas were to them just five lines in an Excel-sheet'.

This is how innovation cultures die. As TS Eliot would have it in *The Hollow Men*, 'Not with a bang but a whimper'.

## The whimper

It is important to note what we can say about this case and what we cannot. Obviously it is only the story of one man, albeit a very senior person in the organization. But it is also a telling story of how decay sets in and starts eating away at a creative culture. By first inspiring and then disenchanting a person, the company managed to achieve the opposite of what it set out to do, at least in this one case. Now imagine it wasn't just one person, but five. Then imagine their disenchantment leads to them treating others in the organization with less respect, each over time disenchanting five more each. And then imagine – 5, 25, 125, 625, 3,125, 15,625… Now imagine it's not starting now, but started many years ago. In your own company.

A 'broken windows' approach to understanding innovation culture assumes that innovation isn't just something that is plugged into a culture by way of a workshop or an initiative. Instead, a more holistic approach is needed. Innovation cultures are things that need to be continuously tended. Things such as fatigue or killing ideas by yawning is something that can occur at almost any time, even invisibly.

*Innovation cultures are things that need to be continuously tended.*

In the example above, it is not the case than anyone set out to insult the man I met by the lifts. On the contrary, the executive team set out to raise spirits and enhance innovation. What they forgot to take into account were the little things. The Excel-sheet created for the idea competition was in all likelihood a task that was farmed off to some relatively low-ranking member of the administrative staff. He or she probably never thought about communication and feedback as they tallied the ideas. The person who sent out the emails probably did exactly as they were told, which was to email everyone who had submitted an idea – without looking for duplicates.

Ideas in the modern corporation tend to die a death of a thousand cuts, and the same goes for innovation cultures. The tricky thing is that we sometimes cannot even see the cuts.

## How to kill innovation culture with an idea competition, part 2

The story of the ill-fated idea competition didn't stop there, either. I ended up travelling to the finale, which was held in a magnificent castle in Eastern Europe. In a large ballroom, all gold fittings and burgundy velvet, the top leadership of the company had gathered to listen to the six shortlisted ideas. After a light buffet lunch, the show was about to begin. The ballroom had a stage, from where the ideas were to be pitched, and most people sat on chairs arranged in straight rows, as at so many other corporate events. I say most, as the jury for the idea competition, which consisted of the executive team without the CEO (who didn't think the CEO should be judging, but who also was in the audience), sat in a flattened semicircle arranged so that it was directly in front of the slightly rotated podium. I sat next to the CEO in the front row, to the right of the jury semicircle.

The first presentation was delivered by a dapper man who bore a striking resemblance to a successful junior partner in a top consulting firm. His suit was flawless, his tie narrow, his presentation slick, and he had a very confident style about him. He delivered his idea in a most professional manner, continuously speaking to the jury and inviting them to comment. Nothing. The executive team, who had now sat down comfortably, did listen, but did not otherwise move a muscle. They sat, most of them in closed and dismissive positions, and looked not unlike a herd of water buffalo, staring at the young man. As his presentation went on, his confidence seemed to leave him, as did his smile. Towards the end he still smiled bravely and ended with a 'Questions?' Nothing. Nothing whatsoever. After a quick thank you, he scuttled off.

The second presentation was delivered by a young woman, who was neither as snappily dressed nor as professional a presenter as the previous finalist. Her slide deck was decidedly more amateurish, and she didn't exude professionalism so much as a bubbly kind of joy to be on stage. She presented, with passion and gusto, but also openly worked the jury, trying to coax a smile or similar out of them. Nothing. Nothing at all. She soldiered on, bravely, and as she got to the end she too invited questions from the jury. Not a sound.

At this point I was somewhat agitated and elbowed the CEO, hissing 'Do something!' to him. He, bewildered, said 'What?' I repeated that he should do something and continued 'You've asked me how innovation fails in organizations? Well, you're looking at it!' What was supposed to be the company's big celebration of ideas was quickly coming apart, and people were squirming slightly in their seats. The CEO listened and then said, 'Well, what can I do?' with a shrug. Almost apoplectic at this point I reminded him that he was the CEO, and it was in his power to do quite a few things, such as straighten out his executive team, or end the farce that was playing out before us before things got even more embarrassing.

By now the third presenter had already gotten on stage, but by now something had changed in the jury, and the entire audience could notice the change. One person from the executive team had nodded off and was by now snoring softly. When I think back, it sounded a little like windows cracking.


## Shallow yawns and deep breaths

These stories all illustrate two intertwined phenomena in contemporary organizations. One, they are illustrations about how common it is that ideas die not from active criticism, but rather from a lack of care and engagement. Two, they aim to communicate that it isn't enough to just want your company to be more innovative. You may have spent a fortune on your innovation initiative, but an execution that communicates a fundamental lack of care for ideas can make this backfire and make your organization *less* innovative than more so for it. You cannot create a culture hospitable to ideas simply by putting up motivational posters and running a few workshops, if the lived reality of the organization is one of yawns, lack of engagement and the metaphoric broken windows.

What is at play here is a continuation of the shallow innovation cultures referred to in the introduction. In the examples here, there was lip-service paid to innovation, even funds for new ideas. But they also show a fundamental lack of understanding for the deeper nature of innovation cultures. These companies didn't lack ideas, just as I said that no company does so. On the contrary, the chemical company proved to be bursting at the seams with ideas and with people who were prepared to spend nights and weekends to develop the same. The Sphinx-like manager had, just in the short time I observed him in meetings, been presented with quite a few ideas, despite his dismissive demeanour. I have seen variations of this play out in more than a hundred companies, with differing intensity and in varying ways, but always so that the assumed lack of ideas wasn't a lack at all. What was lacking can be referred to in different ways – care, engagement, a supportive culture, reciprocity – but the story is always the same. Ideas are introduced and then ignored; over time the innovation culture first withers, then dies. This can be formulated as the key lesson I've drawn from studying both innovation successes and innovation failures in several hundred companies:

*The number one thing required for innovation is not ideas, but a supportive culture.*

We will go into this in more detail in the next chapter, so for now suffice it to say that such a culture is less defined by how much it can repeat the mantras of shallow innovation and more by the way in which it can deeply embody a care for and an engagement with ideas – even ideas that seem strange, even ludicrous at first. Here, deep innovation refers to deep support, on having a culture that tends to its broken windows and makes sure that ideas aren't yawned at. But to build such deep support, we first need to look inside.

## Our own worst enemies

When I lecture on creativity and innovation in companies, I often start by highlighting a curious fact about the way people think about their own abilities when it comes to creativity. Some creativity consultants I've had the misfortune to listen to make a big deal out of the fact that when asked, close to 100 per cent answer that creativity is important to the work that they do – and this holds true no matter if you ask senior researchers or data entry clerks. In fact, I've noticed a slight tendency for people to be more keen to answer yes to such a question if they perceive others think their jobs are non-creative. If you ask accountants, they are often the first to put their hands up if the question is asked... But this answer is not very interesting in itself. We are obviously all keen to be seen to be productive employees and wish for others to see us in a favourable light, so it is actually quite unlikely anyone would willingly speak of themselves or their work as wholly without creativity.[6]

When you ask people whether they see themselves as particularly creative, another, slightly more interesting, pattern emerges. Only a very few will immediately put themselves forward as being extra creative, and it has been my experience that a significant portion of those who do are seen as quarrelsome rather than creative by their peers. A similar minority will state that they are not particularly creative. Again, some of their peers will challenge this, even to the point where I've seen a fight erupt over one person's creativity, where she herself downplayed her capacities and another aggressively insisting she was 'the most creative person here'. Various things can influence such tendencies to portray oneself or others as an outlier, but the key point to observe here is that people rarely speak of themselves as occupying an extreme point on the creativity scale.

For most groups, the defining pattern is one well known in the social sciences. It harks back to the well-known 80/20 split that often occurs when analysing bigger data sets. There are many rules of thumb that have emerged around this split (sometimes referred to as the Pareto principle), so that we often assume that 20 per cent of customers generate 80 per cent of sales, 20 per cent of employees will generate 80 per cent of complaints, and so on. When studying things such as perceived capability, another version of this comes into play, one where we as a group overestimate these. For instance, 80 per cent of people think that they are better drivers than average, even though this is mathematically impossible. The same goes for the 80 per cent of people who think they are better looking than the average. In creativity, something very similar occurs. About 80 per cent of people (the exact figure varies from study to study, but every test I've run with groups I've worked with has landed approximately here) see themselves as more creative than average, if only slightly so.[7] This can, again, be explained by our innate desire to view ourselves in at least a moderately positive light.

Things get really interesting, however, when you move away from whether people are or aren't creative, shifting the question and thereby the perspective. In some of the large-scale projects I've done with companies regarding creative capabilities and innovation cultures, I've started by mapping the company or unit with both pilot interviews and a questionnaire. In the latter, I've always included a question (at times with duplicate questions to test for validity) regarding how capable people are of recognizing creative ideas, in their field or in general. In other words, not whether they're capable of generating them but recognizing one when they come across it. The results tend to be astonishing. When I've formulated it as a yes/no question, i.e. 'I can recognize when someone suggests a creative idea in my field', the results often get up to 98 per cent positive replies. When using something like a seven-level Likert scale, I've often obtained about 90 per cent clustering around the two strongest positives. In both cases, these are exceptional results. What they indicate, and what creativity research long has known, is that we might at times be bashful or uncertain regarding our own creative mojo. *But we are absolutely sure we know creativity when we see it.*

*We are absolutely sure we know creativity when we see it.*

The problem? It's just not true. Not even close. In fact, the history of innovation is filled with cases where specifically those who were supposed to have expertise in a field failed to recognize ideas as being creative when they first came across them. As Youngme Moon details in her delightful *Different: Escaping the competitive herd*,[8] the typical reaction to innovative approaches tends to be one of incomprehension. As an example, she details Google's homepage. When this was first launched, the usual search page was a crowded page of links, sports scores, weather and whatever else might be fitted onto it. Google's homepage was austere, with only a logo, a search box and two buttons, and in fact so different that according to Moon, the most common response to it in the beginning was to reload it, as the page seemed to have loaded incorrectly! This is telling, for this is actually how we tend to react to creative ideas – with incredulity, if not amusement or out-and-out hostility.

## The beam in our eyes

I like to illustrate the same point by asking my audiences to imagine their industry – regardless of what industry they are in.

Then I ask them a few (arguably very leading) questions. I ask if service is important in their industry, and they all nod in assent. I ask if they aim to deliver the product or service the customers want, and they say 'Yes', often with a slightly puzzled look on their faces – as the question seems so silly. I ask them if they aim to take good care of their customers, and again everyone is in agreement.

Now picture it, I tell them, a new entrant comes into the market. They have the same technology as everyone else, but a very different approach. They start by announcing that service is for losers. They will aim for no service at all. In fact, they'll *penalize* customers who need service. They also declare that they intend to be the least customer-centric company known to humankind. In fact, they say, they intend to torture their customers, whenever they're not busy fleecing them. Oh, and their pledge will be to never, ever give the customer exactly what they want but often something far from what they actually wanted. Oh, and they intend to be ridiculously successful when doing this.

At this point, the audience is often laughing to themselves. It sounds so silly, so provably impossible as an idea. No-one could manage in that manner! When I tell them that this isn't just a test, this is an actual description of a successful business case, some in the audience look genuinely flustered. Some of my readers may have figured it out already. It is of course the story of Ryanair (or, more precisely, the revamping of Ryanair's service at the beginning of the 1990s). Proud of being a no-frills airline, they have gone to some lengths to minimize service, and their fees for those who need to get service with a bag are legendary. Their business model is built on maximal cost-cutting and aggressive extra monetization, and the company has publicly floated the idea of charging for using toilets on board and installing 'standing seats' for those willing to forgo sitting down during a flight as a needless luxury.[9]

This example should not be read as a criticism of Ryanair; quite the contrary. I use it as an example of how an industry can miss out on opportunities that seem self-evident in retrospect. When Ryanair was first announced, the entire airline industry scoffed – when they weren't chuckling. Everyone knew that such a business model could never work, and whilst it was 'different', it most certainly wasn't creative. Or so they thought. Looking back we can of course see that low-cost airlines revolutionized the market and that there was a huge amount of customers that were prepared to endure minimal service and airports far from their intended destination, as long as the price was right.

It is indicative of the innovation industry that Ryanair is seldom used as an example. This is not because it didn't have an innovative approach – it did. This is not because Michael O'Leary hasn't been creative, because he has. It is because Ryanair doesn't live up to the aesthetic ideals of shallow innovation culture. It doesn't *look* like an innovation, and therefore many innovation pundits have decided to ignore it. Just like many in my audiences, who self-assuredly nod along to statements about service and being customer-centric, and chuckle when I talk about torturing customers as a business model, ignore possible ideas simply because they do not fit with their preconceived notions.

I end my little tale by saying that it is easy to laugh at the big airlines who didn't realize just how impactful low-cost airlines would be. But we are more like them than we'd like to admit. We nod where we think we should nod and laugh when something challenges this. And what if their industry's Ryanair-idea is already here? What if it actually has been aired at this company? What if you, being an expert and all, already killed it?

## The curse of expertise

Innovation history teaches us that human beings are terrible at identifying innovative ideas. Almost every creative idea or technology was initially laughed at – the iPhone and the internet, today iconized by the innovation industry, were both initially panned by experts – and there is no telling how many ideas with great potential were killed long before they had a chance to prove themselves. We can see this happening on a macro-scale, where governments and corporations often play catch-up when it comes to revolutionary technological shifts, and we can see it happening on a micro-scale such as in the innovation competition described earlier. It happens

*Innovation history teaches us that human beings are terrible at identifying innovative ideas.*

because whilst we think we are highly adept at recognizing creativity, we are in fact not very good at it at all. As curious as it sounds, the better we are at something and the more expertise we've amassed, the worse we often get.

Take Uber, for instance. In 2017, amongst rumours of a toxic working culture, the new CEO Dara Khosrowshahi gave his first public interview, at the DealBook Conference. In this, he admitted that the company had problems and identified the root cause of these as being a somewhat surprising culprit: winning. He stated that the fantastic growth and success of the company had created a culture in which some saw bad behaviour as acceptable, almost as spoils of war, and went on to say that whilst Uber had grown, 'it wasn't necessarily scaling in terms of culture'. Some might say that this is too simple an answer (many other companies have grown rapidly without being known for boisterous antics and sexual harassment), but there is also truth here. Cultures do not necessarily scale at the same speed as a company does, and success can easily breed arrogance.

With a culture filled with experts, i.e. people with a thorough historical understanding of an area, this can be further enhanced, particularly when it comes to new ideas and innovative approaches. As people become experts due to their historical success in a field, this also means they become invested in the selfsame success. As experts gravitate to experts, this investment becomes part of the culture, an endowment to be protected. As in the justly famous studies on endowment bias by psychologists Amos Tversky and Daniel Kahneman, where people were shown to overestimate the value of what they already owned, amassed expertise will often be overvalued over new ideas.

For an eye-opening example of this, consider the case of Somersby Cider, a premium line from Carlsberg, one of the world's biggest breweries. When originally suggested, the idea of extending into a decidedly non-beer drink was both passively and actively resisted in the organization. Many of the key people in the organization had a long history with brewing beer, with more than a few being brewers themselves (something that was an internal point of pride). Implicitly and explicitly they suggested that there was no point in going to such a 'girly' drink, and there were great misgivings about the size of the market. Such was the resistance that, according to the person I interviewed, the money given for the pilot project was seen as a way of silencing the person who championed Somersby, as it was widely believed the experiment would fail. It didn't. In fact, its success came as a shock to the company, as it turned into one of the most successful launches ever for Carlsberg.[10]

Here, it would be easy to laugh at the brewers who failed to see the value of the idea and accuse them of being blinkered. Still, this is in all likelihood the wrong lesson. Instead, we should be aware that we too carry similar biases, grounded in our experience and expertise, and rather ask ourselves how one can build an organization that is resilient in the face of endowment bias, one that can move from passively killing ideas to actively nurturing the same.

## Beyond innovation theatre

Whilst you might think that all organizations have a genuine interest in developing, the fact of the matter is that when it comes to innovation, many organizations primarily engage in playacting. Steve Blank, the startup maven and the father of the lean startup methodology, has used the term *innovation theatre* to describe the way in which major corporations try to gain cachet by emulating startup techniques.[11] Such initiatives can take many forms but often involve setting up a small entity that is to symbolize a new-found innovative spirit in the corporation. Blank's scornful depiction of this as 'theatre' is based on the fact that such projects often end up as little more than PR exercises and that the entities are rarely afforded the resources or the power to actually achieve very much. The real decision-making power, as well as the critical resources, usually stay with the traditional, 'safe' parts of the organization, and whilst the innovation exercises may put up a good show, little actually changes.

Where Blank uses the term specifically to berate the manner in which big corporations play startup games, a very similar critique can be directed to innovation initiatives more generally. These are, by and large, more focused on showing off that one 'does innovation' than on actual change and, as a result, are very tied up in the histrionics of it all. Join any one innovation workshop, seminar, competition, or the like, and you are likely to come across the very same stage-setting and many of the same lines.

How does one start to combat this? Simply put, through a three-part methodology:

*Acknowledge the problem, build a support system, grow from a deeper place.*

We will look into this in the following chapter. We will look at why leaders need to think like farmers, why a lack of civility can signal big trouble for innovation, and why you can't have creativity without generosity.

# CHAPTER THREE

# Respect, reciprocity, responsibility and reflection

*Crafting innovation cultures from the ground up*

*'For good ideas and true innovation, you need human interaction, conflict, argument, debate.'*
MARGARET HEFFERNAN

## Why innovation requires thinking like a farmer

The world culture comes from the Latin *cultus*, which can be translated as 'care' or 'cultivation' but also 'worship'. As a word, culture is also connected to the French *colere*, which means 'to till'. All in all, the concept of culture stems from notions of planting and harvesting, tending the earth, agriculture. This is of course not the same as saying that hunter-gatherers lacked a culture of their own (they didn't) but that culture has a deep connection with caring and nurturing for something. We can see this in the manner in which a community cares for a building that holds special importance for them, or in the importance of educating and nurturing the young. To have a culture is to have a foundation upon which things can be built and a community around these things that aims to preserve and tend to them. Whilst it might sound self-evident, even trivial, what this means is that a culture is a cultivated, cared-for thing.

It is therefore surprising how little attention is often paid to care and nurturing when discussing innovation cultures. Often, if culture is even addressed, this is done in a way that emphasizes things like risk-taking and experimentation, and if care is even addressed, it is under headings such as 'not punishing failure'. Talk of innovation cultures often focuses on things such as 'mavericks' and 'skunkworks', further enhancing the image of innovation as something special and something reserved for a select few. In practice, attention to innovation cultures very often pivots towards an interest in successful innovation projects. Were we to use farming terms, we would still talk of innovation cultures as if the only important thing was whether a farmer has a prize-winning stallion or not, rather than looking to the farm itself.

But as any farmer knows, this is madness. In order to have a healthy farm, you need to tend to the soil, feed all the chickens (and not just the rooster) and, above all, pay most attention when things are at their tenderest. Without a sense of care for first shoots and newborn piglets, a farmer will quickly become an ex-farmer.

Switching back to innovation terms, we've seen in the previous chapter how ideas often die when they are mere tender shoots. An organization culture that doesn't show care for budding innovations at this stage cannot become an innovation culture, simply because it will not be nurturing and supportive enough. Just like you cannot plant seeds into ground that is rock hard and hasn't been tilled, you cannot ignore the culture within which ideas either live or die – and no amount of theatre will change this. Instead, building a deep innovation culture starts from something very simple: *psychological safety*.

## PS I love you

The desire to feel safe is one of the most fundamental ones for human beings, and we are hardwired to react to threats to this safety. Things like fight-or-flight responses or your heart rate elevating in situations that feel unsafe are well known to most of us. We also innately know how important it is for humans to feel psychologically safe in our private lives, so that we can trust our partners and our close friends. It might seem curious that this fact, which is self-evident to most people (at least when addressed), has been neglected in a lot of the writing on our professional lives – and even more so in the writings on innovation culture.

The term 'psychological safety' as it relates to workplaces is commonly attributed to Amy Edmonson, who introduced it to describe a positive state in work teams, one where all the individuals in the team feel that they can voice their ideas and opinions without fearing censure or dismissive behaviour. Or, in the more stilted terms of her 1999 article[1] 'a shared belief held by members of the team that the team is safe for interpersonal risk taking'. Simply put, when people feel that they don't need to be afraid to raise an issue or present an idea, teams work better. This might seem like a most obvious observation, but as anyone who has worked in a less than nurturing group can attest to, it is not always a state we reach.

Google, in one of the biggest studies ever done on the inner workings of efficient teams – Project Aristotle[2] – followed Edmonson's cue and found it even more impactful than she originally suggested. In fact, after intense study of their own teams, Google's researchers came to the conclusion that psychological safety was possibly the most important indicator of an efficient team. Whilst things such as interpersonal friendships or having a strong leader did little to nothing to predict whether a group was efficient or not, psychological safety had a massive correlation to efficiency.

The research conducted in Project Aristotle came up with further insights into the making of psychological safety and highlighted two interrelated processes. One was that efficient teams had a high level of social sensitivity, i.e. when people in a team are good at picking up on signals about how others in the team feel, this improves psychological safety. The second, arguably more interesting, finding was that psychological safety could be at least approximately measured by 'equality in distribution of conversational turn-taking'. What this means is that teams in which people speak in more or less equal measure outperform those where a select few dominate the discussion. Whilst a logical extension of the model of psychological safety, it also gives us a way to quickly gauge the psychological safety in our own organization. Just observe your next meeting; does everyone contribute, and is everyone listening to everyone else?

What is now important to note is that these observations function beyond the boundaries of work teams, can be addressed on a cultural level and have an impact on a company's capacity to innovate.

## Psychological safety, innovation and organizational culture

Psychological safety in both teams and the organization is critical for establishing a support system for ideas. Psychological safety is very rarely raised in the literature on innovation. As we saw in the last chapter, organizations can, despite professing to care deeply about innovation, at the same time be hotbeds for behaviours and micro-behaviours that decrease or demolish psychological safety. In a similar fashion, the fatiguing effects of endless innovation workshops and calls to superficial innovation literature can create patterns in organizations that

*Psychological safety is critical for establishing a support system for ideas.*

make people less likely to engage with the conversation. In order to start building a new, deeper innovation culture, we thus need to find the patterns that reignite people's desire to engage and affirm a sense of psychological safety around innovation. Somewhat more succinctly put, we need to make people feel safe and supported in discussing it all – including raising criticisms against shallow innovation when needed.

The thing with psychological safety is that it is easy to grasp and like but difficult to establish. A culture in which people have become accustomed to yawns and dismissals when it comes to new ideas will not automatically become nurturing just because management says that 'psychological safety' is important. On the contrary, such statements may well feed into a cultural belief that 'innovation talk' is superficial and something to be (easily) ignored.

Consider, instead, what I experienced in a German corporation that had battled with shallow and show-off innovation for a long period of time. The CEO, who had subconsciously been aware of this for quite a while, became very animated after I gave a keynote speech at an internal event in the company. As a result of being somewhat provoked by the other keynote speaker, I had launched into a tirade against shallow innovation, and as the CEO joined me on stage he declared that these were his exact sentiments regarding what was going on in the company. I later learnt that he'd taken somewhat extreme measures in relation to this. In the weeks that followed, he instituted a policy in which using the word 'innovation' was forbidden in internal communication. The word was still liberally used in marketing and reports shared externally, but the CEO decreed that no use of it would be allowed in-house, in neither written nor spoken form. This probably sounds quite extreme to most people, but the results were quite interesting. Whilst originally treated as something of a joke, the move went on to change the organization's mode of talking about new projects and investments, with employees reporting a distinct change in how many participated in the discussion on these. It seemed that the instituted change in language had quelled at least some of the discursive excesses amongst management and had given people who previously experienced being excluded from discussions about new projects a chance to participate.

Building a support system for psychological safety and through this for innovation, is thus not just a question of stating the importance of a new value or instituting new innovative management processes. Instead, it requires a number of engagements, sometimes even strange-sounding ones (like the one earlier), to ensure a culture where the full cognitive surplus of the organization is engaged with. In the following section, we'll delve a little deeper into what this requires.

## Some hallmarks of an innovation culture

The challenge of innovation cultures lies not in the aspects that are easy to grasp but in the one's that are easy to overlook. As researchers in organizational culture have long argued, the most important thing about these are the assumptions about the world that the organization often subconsciously holds, as well as the values that the organization lives through its practices. An organization may well claim to value things like individuality and risk-taking, yet hold onto assumptions about the importance of mitigating all risks and have values that emphasize consensus – as anyone who has ever worked in the finance industry can attest to.

In innovation, this can play out in several ways. Central to what we're talking about here is to look for the elements of a supportive innovation culture, beyond the shallow prescriptions of the innovation industry. To recap, the elements that are most often referred to when attempting to build a culture of innovation in an organization are:

1   an openness to ideas, both internal and external;
2   freedom to experiment and a culture of learning;
3   a tolerance for risk and failures;
4   processes to develop talents and ideas;
5   making resources available and establishing metrics.

Whilst these are important aspects, they presuppose a number of things, such as there being a fundamental psychological safety in place so that people voice ideas, and a culture in which engaging with innovation is seen as meaningful. What is needed before issues such as processes and metrics, is an environment where ideas and people are treated with respect.


## The four Rs of deep innovation cultures

In my research, a few themes come up over and over again. One is the tendency for companies to be enthralled with shallow innovation and the products of the innovation industry. Another is the belief that whatever company I'm working with is currently struggling with having too few good ideas – when often the opposite is true. For our purposes here, however, another series of observations are more important. In trying to establish what truly sets innovation cultures apart and what makes some go far deeper than others, it turns out that the earlier list is not very helpful. Most companies try to be open to new ideas, have a tolerance for failure, encourage experimentation and so on. Yet only some succeed, and very few succeed in making this something that truly drives change. The interesting thing is that there are similarities in those that do and elements that are repeated between them.

After more than a decade working with these issues, I've whittled it down to four interrelated elements or cultural values that define deep innovation cultures. Not so that all deep innovation cultures have them in equal measure, or that one needs to be equally strong in all of these, but a lack of any one of these is often a clear signal that a company's innovation culture is in trouble. The four elements/values are, in a loosely coupled order:

1 *respect*;
2 *reciprocity*;
3 *responsibility*;
4 *reflection*;

Each one of these will deepen the prerequisite psychological safety in an organization, and each will in turn create additional engagements in the innovation culture of a corporation. Together, they form a whole that takes the basic psychological safety of well-functioning organizations and makes it possible to embed innovation in a deeper and more meaningful fashion therein. Once the culture is engaged on this level, the organization can then grow from this deeper place. It will also be far less likely to engage in innovation theatre, be beset by innovation fatigue, or passively kill off ideas. Over time, it will also capture more and more of the cognitive surplus of the organization – as long as they are continuously worked with as values – and become better at utilizing the innate imagination and creativity of the organization. I will now go through each of these in turn, but it should be noted that they of course both overlap and interact.

## Respect: the basic building block of innovation

If there is one concept, one word, that encapsulates the foundation of a healthy innovation culture, it is ***respect***. It might sound like a soft and fuzzy word, one more suitable for meditations on HR and diversity practices than innovation, but this is a dangerous fallacy. In the preceding chapter we saw how a lack of respect could make a person swear to never share ideas again, and this is sadly not an isolated incident. In more than 80 per cent of the companies where I've identified problems in their innovation culture, people explicitly or implicitly communicated that they didn't feel that their ideas or inputs got the respect that they felt they deserved, which directly led to innovation fatigue. Christine Porath, through a survey including more than 20,000 people worldwide, found that respect was the number one leadership behaviour employees wish for, but also that people increasingly report feeling disrespected in the workplace.[3]

Although we all instinctively understand the concept, this doesn't mean respect is easy to define. Respect can be simply described as the act of treating people in a manner that takes their feelings into consideration, or acting in a manner that communicates regard for another person. This can be done in a more implicit manner, for instance by simply listening to each person in a meeting, or in a more explicit one, such as when one commends an employee in a visible fashion. Importantly, respect is much like trust in that it might be more easily noticed by its absence. We are exceptionally good at noticing when respect is lacking. Think for instance about when a boss refuses to acknowledge your presence or when your name isn't listed when contributors to a project are thanked despite your input (both cases I've experienced in my research, and both cases where this demoralized the person who felt disrespected). This is in part due to the fact that basic respect is part of the social contract, the way in which we humans interact. To notice a lack of respect is thus to notice that social rules are breached, which is why we often react very strongly to it.

However, respect isn't just an issue of people. This is the dimension we're most used to thinking and talking about, but particularly in the field of innovation where the way in which ideas can be met with either respect or disrespect is hugely important. You cannot capture the cognitive surplus of an organization if you've primed people not to share it, and you cannot create meaning in an organization where people do not even respect each other.

## Embedding respect: a guide for leaders

So how do you go about making a culture respectful? How can a leader (and note that I'm not talking here just about bosses and formal leaders but about everyone who wants to enact meaningful change in an organization) make respect into a cultural value? First, by realizing that this isn't done overnight. Respect is a cultural value that can take a long time – even years – to properly institute. In other words, this kind of cultural transformation requires vigilance and patience. Second, leaders need to start this by looking to the kinds of behaviours that can embed a culture of respect into an organization. In my research on innovation cultures, four behaviours stand out as central to achieving this, and we look now at each of these in turn.

*Respect is a cultural value that can take a long time – even years – to properly institute.*

**Lead by example.** No organization will embrace respect unless its leaders, including those at the very top, are prepared to show the same. In each engagement with ideas from employees, customers or collaborators, leaders need to show that they take these seriously and are prepared to engage with them. Sometimes it can be as easy as asking a follow-up question; at other times it may require setting up an exploratory project. In all cases, leaders need to start by showing respect if they wish others to do so.

**Allow civil dissent.** Respect isn't all about being nice. It is also about allowing people to voice dissenting opinions and creating a space for the same. Psychological safety starts this process, but it is only if a culture becomes used to having respectful discussions about matters where their opinions diverge that respect can become rooted. By practising simultaneous dissent and respect, i.e. tolerance and civility towards those with other ideas, a culture becomes ever better at respect.

*Reward kindness*. As respect and civility seem like 'just good manners', they are often noticed only in their absence. In order to turn this around, leaders should incentivize things such as being kind to co-workers and their ideas. Taking the time to ask follow-up questions on the ideas of others may to some seem like a waste of time, especially if there is no clear cultural signal that it isn't. A leader wishing to develop an innovation culture should thus think not only about the people with the ideas but the ones who nurture and develop them.

*Consider the little things*. Respect is no one thing. As previously stated, a badly timed yawn can easily kill an idea. If a leader truly wishes to craft a respect culture, s/he needs to pay attention to how small things – micro-behaviours – can either support people's feelings of psychological safety and a nurturing environment, or blight it. Consider the words used, body-language, minute changes in affect. Innovation is built not only by big ideas but small, respectful gestures.

## Respecting ideas

One of the core things people get wrong about creativity and innovation in organizations is that they confuse respect and vapidity. Consider the following example (developed from notes taken when working with a pharmaceutical giant). During a project meeting, two individuals suggest ideas for developing a diagnostics tool. The first one to speak is someone we will call Samantha, and her idea is received with friendly smiles as well as a follow-up question. The second person to pitch an idea is Peter, whose idea is met with more than one furrowed brow and several questions, two of which are rather critical. Now, which of these ideas was met with more respect?

You could argue that Samantha's idea got a warmer reception, but this would be to misunderstand how ideas work in organizations. Many women would probably instinctively recognize what happened. Samantha's idea met a modicum of respect – silence as she spoke, people signalling that they were happy to let her suggest an idea – but the idea itself wasn't. Peter's idea, whilst meeting more resistance, was in a very real way respected more than Samantha's. Whilst Samantha may have got the smiles, it was Peter's idea that was taken seriously. Yes, there were critical questions, but we should be careful not to confuse criticism with disrespect. In fact, when it comes to ideas, criticism is often a sign of respect. Peter's idea was met with interest (furrowed brows rather than bland smiles), and people immediately started engaging with it. Even the more critical questions actually worked in the idea's favour, as they enabled Peter to develop and hone his pitch. It should come as little surprise that it was this idea that survived the meeting and went on to become a proper development project, whereas Samantha's idea didn't.

What we can find in deep innovation cultures is thus often a double move when it comes to respect. There needs to be a fundamental respect in the culture, one that nurtures psychological safety and makes people feel that they can present ideas without risk of censure or humiliation. This is the foundation. In addition to this there needs to be a culture in which ideas are respected – and engaged with.

## Critique considered as one of the fine arts

As previously stated, one of the reasons many corporations struggle with innovation is because they do not represent a hospitable context for ideas. Part of such a context is psychological safety; part is a culture of *productive criticism*. If we look to some of the most famous cases of creative organizations, one thing that stands out is just how good these are at constantly critiquing their own work. We have all heard the stories of Steve Jobs as an arch-critic, continuously exhorting his staff to do better; similar stories are today told of Jeff Bezos. Pixar is famous for endless rounds of inquisitive questioning regarding all aspects of its movies, and anyone who has worked in a top ad agency can attest to the atmosphere of querying criticism that defines these. In my own work with creative organizations, I've often been blown away at the capacity for critique they are capable of – as the next story illustrates.

Relatively early in my career I had the chance to spend some time at a UK ad agency, where I was conducting what is known as 'shadowing' (a method where you observe the goings-on in an organization without actively participating or interviewing people). On the very first day, I got to sit in as a small group was supposed to go through a campaign idea that was to be pitched to a client a week later. The meeting started, somewhat abruptly, by a man walking in and demonstratively slapping the draft document onto the table. He then went on to detail his take on it, and his take was not positive. Quite the contrary. He absolutely trashed the idea, engaged in very creative cursing and suggested that the lead person who'd done the draft was an idiot. He rebutted these criticisms, with no small amount of foul language, after which the conversation became a veritable screaming match. After half an hour of intense arguing, where I was fairly sure a punch was about to be thrown, the combattants quietened down. Both were standing by a whiteboard at this point but sat down as if on cue and suddenly broke into huge smiles. Gathering their things, they walked out of the room, happily chitchatting. I was quite confused at this point. A junior team-member turned to me and went, 'Yeah, it can be a bit strange if you're not used to it. They're best mates, you see. This is how they work, savaging one others' ideas, and they just make each other better'.

Whilst such capacity for giving and taking no-holds-barred criticism might be rare, productive criticism is something that most if not all organizations can develop improved skills in. The core issue here is to understand that engaging with ideas is a sign of respect. It signals that you've listened to the person coming up with the idea, that you've cared enough to think about his or her idea and that you are prepared to engage with the person who came up with it. It is often said that the opposite of love isn't hate, but indifference, which is why a couple can fight like cat and dog and still have a healthy relationship. Organizations, however, often fall into the trap of indifference and simply do not work enough on their critiquing skills.

To strengthen such, leaders need to consider three things.

One, leaders need to ensure that every raised idea receives, at a minimum, some feedback and questions. Productive criticism is like any other skill and only develops if continuously worked on. By instituting policies that ensure that people will always get at least the courtesy of a response, an organization can ensure that people at least won't feel disrespected in the process.

Two, leaders need to demand that all criticism be qualified. Blanket condemnations such as 'that'll never work' should never be allowed unless accompanied with serious argument *why* the proposed idea wouldn't work. This makes people invest more thought into their critiques and also moves the conversation towards argumentation rather than definite judgement.

Three, people should always be afforded the right to respond. Sure, your idea may have been harshly criticized, but at least you got the opportunity to fight for it. As strange as it may seem, people are generally happier to have an idea shot down if they feel that they were given a fair chance to defend it – as is seldom the case in shallow innovation cultures.

Deep innovation cultures pride themselves on dialogue and productive criticism and ensure that there is an ongoing, critical but respectful discussion about ideas. They understand that getting yawned at can often be more hurtful than getting tough questions.

## The power of civility

The trouble with criticism in the workplace is that in order to be efficient it needs to be both productive and civil, and often it is neither. I have already referred to Christine Porath's research on this – for a good summation I recommend her *Mastering Civility:*

*A manifesto for the workplace*[4] – where she argues that a lack of civility sabotages both productivity and health in modern organizations. With more than half of those she polled stating that they weren't regularly treated with respect by their bosses, it painted a bleak picture of working life today.

At the same time, this all points to there being a simple and straightforward way for companies to start improving their cultures and through this their capacity for innovation. Rather than investing millions into complex consulting projects, leaders can start considering how small changes in the way in which people address and treat each other can rebuild civility in the workplace. This was the case in one of the Nordic retail companies I worked with. The company had struggled with high employee turnover and limited creativity in their offerings, and the new CEO was expected to institute sweeping changes. To the surprise of many, he instead opted for a large 'listening tour' of the company. He visited a large amount of the company's outlets and all of their central offices. At each stop, he made a point of being respectful to the staff, asking detailed questions about their workdays. After each visit, he sent a handwritten note of thanks and made sure to keep up email conversations with some of the staff he met on his tour. When I interviewed him, he stated explicitly that he was doing this not just to be liked but to set a new kind of example. He'd realized that there was a tendency in the company to focus on transactional matters, and he wanted people to feel a sense of pride in the company. By making sure that he behaved in a civil and respectful way, he wanted to make this kind of behaviour the new standard, and he was particularly proud of the fact that, as a result, employees, including those on the shop floors, had started to email him directly with new ideas and suggestions for improvement.

By showing respect and civility to people in the organization, regardless of whether they are seen as 'important' (or, for that matter, 'innovative') or not, we can start rebuilding our innovation cultures simply by ensuring that disrespectful practices become less prevalent. By doing this, we enhance psychological safety and start 'repairing windows' rather than allowing broken ones to be the norm. Whilst this doesn't guarantee all good ideas get recognized, it goes a long way towards capturing more and more of the cognitive surplus of the organization. Who knows, maybe Samantha will get another shot?

*Key takeaway: Without an attitude of respect towards ideas and people, the former won't develop and the latter won't engage.*

## Reciprocity: why you need both give and take

The second element that defines deep innovation cultures is *reciprocity*. Simply put, in deep innovation cultures there is an innate understanding that one cannot simply demand that people innovate, without giving them the support that this requires. Or, to put it more simply, there needs to be both give and take. In many corporations I've worked with, this seemingly self-evident wisdom was in fact something of a surprise, at least to top management. As an example, I at one point worked with a major financial institution, with activities in several countries. It had just announced a major innovation drive and signalled that as part of this they would look to both developing innovative digital solutions in-house and through possible acquisitions. This message had been delivered in a quite forceful manner to the employees, with a clear indication that bonuses would be very closely tied to how engaged individuals were with new innovation projects. In many ways, the initiative was run like a textbook innovation strategy. It had several lines of attack, tried to engage outside actors and incentivized innovation. The results, however, did not emerge as quickly as management had expected. Several of them mentioned a distinct feeling of resistance to the new strategy in the organization.

A few interviews lower down in the hierarchy quickly made clear why this was. Yes, people had got the memo and knew that they were supposed to be 'innovation focused'. They also knew that their bonuses were hinging on displaying such focus. What was also clear to them, however, was that whilst there was an incentive, there was little additional support. None of the people I interviewed stated that they'd been given any budget or even time allocations for innovation activities. On the contrary, they reported that from what they could figure out, they were still supposed to do all the same work and finish all the same reports as before. With little extraneous time, innovation was seemingly something they were expected to do in their time off. They felt the demand, but saw few extra supplies.

Similar stories can be found in many corporations. Companies with deep innovation cultures, however, show a markedly different approach. It seems almost silly to have to point it out, but they have understood a core tenet of how to make things happen. ***The core tenet is if you want more innovation, give people what they need in order to innovate.*** Few things are more clichéd in innovation literature than references to the nigh-mythical '15 per cent rule' at 3M (which stated that employees could freely dedicate 15 per cent of their work-time to experimental projects), but at the same time this holds a lesson. 3M insisted on innovation from its employees, but it also reciprocated on this. A very similar story from Google, where (some) employees are allowed to freely allocate 20 per cent of their time to pet projects, also manages to be oft-repeated and rarely copied.

*The core tenet is if you want more innovation, give people what they need in order to innovate.*

Instead, many companies adopt the strategy of the financial institution above, one where innovation is the demand that keeps demanding. So how can we move beyond this?

## Embedding reciprocity: a guide for leaders

Building reciprocity into the very foundations of a culture can be slightly easier than instituting respect and civility, if only because it is easier to pinpoint. This doesn't make the process trivial, but by focusing on a limited set of behaviours, leaders can ensure that reciprocity becomes an increasingly central value in an organization's culture. Through this, we can also strengthen and deepen innovation cultures, by way of the following:

*Make responses mandatory.* Leaders must ensure that the organizational culture doesn't allow ideas to die by no-one engaging with them. No idea should be seen as so small or unimportant that it doesn't get any feedback. Be it on a micro-level, where a leader insists that each proposal in a meeting receives a modicum of questions or comments, or on an organizational level, where suggestions even from the people lowest in a hierarchy get taken seriously, an innovation culture must engage with all ideas. A culture where only the ideas of the few receive responses will always be shallow.

*Promote givers.* Far too many organizations primarily promote takers, those go-getters who are always looking out for number one. In order to build a culture of reciprocity, leaders need to look for the givers of the organization, the people who are always ready to help with comments or support for ideas, and look to promote for generosity. The more givers you have in top management, the easier it will be to build respect and reflection.

*Twin demands with support.* You cannot develop innovation in an organization by simply demanding more and more of it. The issues in corporate innovation rarely stem from people being unaware that innovation is desired, and far more from the fact that employees aren't afforded enough support to experiment with or realize ideas. Leaders wishing to build stronger innovation cultures should make sure that demands are always reciprocated with support – be this allotted time, material resources and/or encouragement.

*Punish indifference.* This is advice I'll probably get in trouble over, as words such as 'punish' aren't really popular in management thinking. I've included this anyway, as I honestly believe that in order to institute reciprocity in an organization, you need to have strong negative incentives when it comes to its very opposite. Deep innovation cultures ensure that indifference is rooted out. They do so by never accepting that people coast by without engaging with or supporting the ideas of others. Sometimes this means pointing out indifferent behaviour in meetings, or in others denying promotions or bonuses to people that simply do not engage with the ideas of others.

## When demands beget defeatism

That said, there are leaders who wholly fail to see this. Once upon a time, in what today seem like halcyon days, it was enough to just be good at your job. Today, employees are often exhorted to be both extremely efficient, constantly learning and, of course, innovative. This last demand is understandable but can, when badly deployed, backfire dramatically. This is because calls for innovation are unique in that they can never be fully satisfied. Whereas we know where the reasonable bounds of efficiency are, innovation has no such bounds – particularly in the discourse of the innovation industry. Here, one can often come across pundits who proudly declare that a 10 per cent improvement is no longer enough and talk excitedly about a '10×' mentality, where employees are exhorted to think of ways to make things ten times better. And why stop there? Why not 100 times better? Or 1,000?!

This might seem like a silly demand to make, but I've actually come across even worse. I at one time consulted the CEO of a maker of fittings and fixtures. He had contacted me after I keynoted a steel conference he'd attended and declared that he saw the very cultural problems I'd addressed in his R&D unit. Here, a group of engineers specialized in plumbing solutions were tasked with creating the future of his company and, as he described things, were failing completely in doing so. I took on the assignment, but after having reviewed their work and interviewed quite a few in the group, I couldn't really see the gross failures the CEO insisted were there. In order to get a better grip on things, I facilitated a meeting between the CEO and the engineers to talk things through. This meeting did not begin well.

Insisting on speaking first, the CEO launched into a diatribe in which he chastised the unit for their failure to come up with 'radical innovations' and for having a mindset that wasn't 'transformational'. Using language that was frankly insulting, he declared that the unit simply wasn't fit for purpose and that it wasn't delivering. Sensing the mood of the room and also picking up on a strange absence in the CEO's speech, I interrupted him. I gently thanked him for speaking his mind but also noted that he was only talking about what the unit *hadn't* done, and that some positive examples might be helpful. For this was the missing element in his speech. He had given no guidance as to what kind of results would be acceptable to him. He sputtered for a moment and then said, 'Well, it's not like I've seen a single Facebook-level idea from this group!'

It took Facebook approximately three years to reach a valuation of US $15 billion. In less than 10, it had a market capitalization of close to US $180 billion. It has grown significantly in value after this. Whilst these are exceptionally impressive figures, their helpfulness in guiding the innovation endeavours of an engineer trying to create better fittings for plumbing are... limited. I suggested this to the CEO and said that the challenges in his innovation strategy might stem more from an expectation mismatch than from a lack of talent amongst his engineers. He scoffed at this, but suddenly people in the R&D unit were energized. One after the other started voicing that they simply didn't know what was expected of them and felt let down and stressed by this. Several indicated that they felt that there was a defeatist culture in the unit, one stemming from the fact that they already knew that they could never live up to the unreasonable demands placed on them. At this point, the CEO was visibly shaken. It had simply not occurred to him that his ill-defined demands might be one of the problems.

## Combatting innovation stress

It is a well-known fact that stress is one of the most damaging aspects of modern work cultures, one that in the United States alone has been estimated to cost companies more than US $300 billion every year from issues such as absenteeism and reduced productivity. Where a small to moderate amount of stress can aid in productivity, even moderate long-term stress affects people's work and health negatively, and ongoing high stress can be linked to everything from decreased creativity to literal death (such as in the Japanese affliction of karōshi – 'overwork death'). Stress, as an affliction, might best be described as stemming from a mismatch between demands placed on a person and the resources (such as time, technology, or other support) that the person is given to meet this demand. If we're given too many tasks and not enough time, we feel stressed.

Curiously, there is little written on *innovation stress*. Besides one article by Cowan *et al.* from 2011,[5] you would be hard-pressed to find it even referenced in the literature. That said, it is not that difficult to find instances of this very real affliction in modern organizations. The reason for this should be glaringly obvious. Innovation is, by its very nature, a risky endeavour with a high degree of uncertainty and where resource-needs can be difficult to predict. It is also a phenomenon with very unequally distributed pay-offs, i.e. some innovation projects can produce astronomical returns whereas most have more limited ones. This can lead to there being exceptionally high expectations on a person or a unit, whilst they themselves may feel they do not have even a fraction of the resources needed for innovation.

In shallow innovation cultures, this can be compounded by innovation theatre, causing people to feel that they are simultaneously asked to achieve the impossible and that their time is often spent playacting innovation rather than engaging seriously with it. In such situations, employees may well become conditioned in a way where even the mention of innovation precipitates a stress reaction. Deep innovation cultures shy away from this and realize that there needs to be a clear reciprocity function at the heart of the innovation strategy, one where demands are balanced with rights and where resourcing is put front and centre. If we for instance look at Koch Industries, the highly successful US industrial conglomerate, their internal process for approving development costs has been lauded for its ease and speed. Investments even in the tens of millions can be approved with a simple phone call, enabling the company to act far faster than competitors with overly cumbersome compliance regimens. In such a culture, the likelihood for deeply rooted innovation stress becomes at the very least alleviated (although other factors may of course affect the overall situation).

## Generosity as an innovation strategy

The psychologist Adam Grant became internationally known with the release of his bestselling *Give and Take: Why helping others drives our success.*[6] In this, he showed that generosity isn't in fact a mug's game, but rather the opposite. Being generous and kind, particularly in the workplace, sets us up for success, for many reasons. In part this is due to the positive influence generous behaviours have, but also because such behaviours resource others, thereby setting you up for reciprocal gains. The term 'win-win' may well be one of the most hated business buzzwords but may well describe generosity as a strategy.

On a cultural level, cultures that value reciprocity draw upon this. They understand that ideas need feedback (which is a form of reciprocity) in order to develop and grow, and they appreciate that resourcing – on many levels – is necessary for there to be meaningful forward action. In other words, the more your culture values giving, be this in the form of feedback or time allotments, the deeper its innovation culture becomes. If respect anchors psychological safety, making people feel not only safe but also valued, reciprocity feeds off it. With both working in concert, a positive spiral of ideas and engagements can be started.

For an example of this, consider Netlight. A fast-growing player in the very competitive realm of IT and management consulting, they are well known for having an award-winning culture as well as being exceptionally profitable. They are also very highly regarded for their level of innovation and the way in which they have executed innovation projects for their clients. Looking to their internal culture (in the interest of full disclosure I should point out that Erik Ringertz, the CEO who has driven the company's growth, is a former student of mine) we can see that reciprocity is at the core of this. The organizational structure emphasizes collaboration, and the culture has strong values when it comes to supporting people. Individuals are seen as having the right to get frank and productive feedback on ideas, as well as resourcing for projects that are seen as worthy of support. Key resourcing decisions are delegated to the culture as a whole, and management can get overruled(!) when it comes to innovation issues. It should come as no surprise that the organization, in addition to being highly profitable, also has sterling Glassdoor-reviews and is considered one of the most attractive places to work in the countries in which it operates.

*Key takeaway: Without reciprocity, in both deeds and resourcing, a culture can't turn ideas into innovations.*

## Responsibility: deep innovation cultures are both vocal and vulnerable

In the introductory chapter of this book I referred to a workshop I ran for a major US corporation, one where I delivered a doggerel version of an innovation lecture. That little intervention had been designed to put the finger on how innovation talk can become so shallow as to become meaningless, but in the conversation I had with the executives I so cruelly tricked, another dimension also emerged. We started to talk about the importance of asking questions, to signal when you do not understand something, and the executives signalled that they often felt the employees accepted things too blithely. I suggested that the problem wasn't just one of shallow innovation talk but also a case of people not taking *responsibility* for their own role in the discussion regarding innovation in the company.

A core reason for many of the innovation ills in shallow innovation cultures is that non-engagement has become acceptable, even the default value. When we observe ideas dying from passivity and a lack of response, what we are in fact seeing is culture where people do not feel that innovation (or engaging with ideas) isn't their responsibility. They may exhibit a baseline civility when new ideas are presented but feel no compunction to participate in the development of the same. This is often seen as a character flaw in employees, particularly amongst top management. I have often heard e.g. CEOs describe their employees with epithets such as 'resistant to change' and 'set in their ways', without them really reflecting on why this is the case.

As previously discussed, experience and expertise can make conservatives of us all. Once we've established a position for ourselves in an organization and a field, we often become prone to defending this position, including defending it from the attack of innovation. Whilst many want to be disrupters, almost no-one wants to be disrupted. This is also why there is such a big market for innovation theatre and shallow innovation books. Rather than truly challenging people's position, they provide pablum that makes it feel like you're engaging in innovation when you are in effect dodging responsibility for the same.

## Embedding responsibility: a guide for leaders

In any organization, there will be a tendency to claim that people within it are already taking responsibility – for their tasks, for their colleagues, for the company. However, a deep innovation culture can only be built when people take responsibility for innovation, the innovation culture and their role in these. In order to build something where this is part of everyday life, rather than something that is claimed in after-dinner speeches, leaders must ensure that there are processes in place to:

*Call nonsense on nonsense.* Each and every organization has its modicum of empty innovation talk. A leader needs to be prepared to call this out, even if this might feel uncomfortable. Unless leaders are prepared to ask pointed questions about shallow innovation, they cannot expect others in the organization to do so. Show responsibility to grow responsibility.

*Respect uncertainty and doubt.* If people express doubt, or feel that the innovation discourse of the organization is exclusive and difficult to live up to, this should be taken seriously. Doubters should never be punished but engaged with. If people express that they feel unsure about their place in an innovation culture, look to what can be done to make them more comfortable with it all. Also consider that not everyone needs to be forced to play innovation games.

*Balance your yin and yang.* Responsibility isn't just about supporting the obvious things. To build a deep innovation culture, a leader needs to look beyond what is normally seen as innovation and take responsibility for bigger wholes. If everyone in the organization is thinking about existing customers, leaders need to bring in the responsibility to think of future customers. If everyone is focused on novelty, the leader needs to remind the organization of the importance of impact.

*Show your insecurities.* Unless leaders are prepared to talk about their own insecurities when it comes to innovation, the organization will not have a real, honest conversation about the same. By being transparent about not understanding a new technology, or by expressing that one doesn't know what 'disruption' really is, a leader can deepen an innovation culture by making it more honest.

## *Staying true, speaking out*

An innovation culture that values responsibility isn't just one where everyone engages with innovation in the prescribed manner. In fact, one might say that the opposite holds true. Amongst the managers who listened to my Dadaist innovation lecture, all felt that they were taking responsibility; they took notes, they listened intently, they tried their best. The only problem was that this was a very flawed notion of responsibility, one where this was understood as just going through the motions. Real responsibility would have been to be prepared to put a hand up and state that one didn't understand – to show vulnerability. This is why working with innovation cultures often requires for us to look for pain points.

I worked at one point with a major Danish technology company, one where the executive team was even more engaged with innovation issues than usual. The company was fairly successful in their endeavours but also very dependent on a few core technologies. As part of a longer engagement, I had run a few workshops with their managers and had picked up on the fact that whilst everyone did dutifully take part, there was a rather large group that seemed to do so in a perfunctory manner. As I felt that this represented a point worth exploring, I started directing a lot of questions to an older gentleman who seemed to be particularly stand-offish with regards to the workshop. Over the course of the day he seemed to get increasingly annoyed, which I used to push him even more (as I felt that the group needed a cathartic reaction). After one last push, he exploded. He started off by claiming that a lot of what we were doing was just empty talk, and as he spoke he got more and more incensed (and, in the Danish manner, very red in the face). He ended up shouting how he hated all the innovation talk he had to engage with, and how he just wanted to do his work and be left out of 'these idiotic games'. As he calmed down and I tried to suppress a smile, I asked how many people agreed with his outburst. More than a third of the group put up their hands.

With this as a backdrop, we redesigned the innovation activities of the organization. Managers were given a choice as to whether they wanted to engage in these or not, which led to far smaller working groups. Interestingly enough, this did not decrease innovation engagement – it increased it! As managers and employees felt that they had the right to opt out, the people who did opt in did so in a far more energetic manner. The ones who opted out became more, not less, likely to support innovation projects and resources for the same. When asked why this was, I suggested that by taking themselves out of the direct innovation work, they still felt it was their responsibility to support those who stuck with it. As innovation no longer seemed like just a compulsory thing for management, more employees took it upon themselves to engage with innovation projects. When I followed up on the project, the CEO even reported that several of those who had originally opted out had by then opted back in, often with far more energy and engagement – including the aggrieved gentleman who initiated the walk-out. As they now felt that it was a choice, taking responsibility for innovation became much easier to do.

## Vulnerability and innovation

What sets deep innovation cultures apart when it comes to responsibility, then, is that they are sensitive to the ways in which employees might (sometimes subconsciously) have conflicting feelings regarding innovation and aim to overcome this. No-one wishes to be seen as anti-innovation, but this is also why we so easily fall into shallow innovation thinking. No-one wishes to sabotage one's own position, and this is why we may keep our mouths shut even when we don't understand something or why we might not wish to engage with ideas that seem to go against our own interests in the organization. Good leaders aim to build cultures where responsibility is paired with notions such as vulnerability and compassion.

Vulnerability has become something of a hot topic in business thinking, thanks to the work of Brené Brown. In her TED-talk (which is one of the most viewed ever) and her bestselling *Daring Greatly: How the courage to be vulnerable transforms the way we live, love, parent, and lead,*[7] she argues that the capacity to show vulnerability and embrace imperfection doesn't weaken a person, a leader or an organization. On the contrary, it is by being honest about our weaknesses that we can build courage and start taking chances.

This said, the notion has not gained a lot of traction in the innovation literature, which despite the occasional homily on failure and risk is still very much tied up in projecting confidence and success. In fact, the innovation industry has something of a history of praising leaders who exhibit almost narcissistic tendencies, or at the very least massive egos. Yet, many of the most successful innovation leaders I've worked with have actually been remarkably humble in the way they discuss innovation internally. I have, for instance, had the opportunity to observe the innovation activities of Konecranes, a global leader in cranes and lifting equipment, particularly under the leadership of Pekka Lundmark (who was CEO from 2005 to 2015). This was a period of sustained growth for the company but also a challenging period during which it became increasingly important to focus on innovation, particularly in the area today best known as IoT/Industry 4.0.

*The innovation industry has something of a history of praising leaders who exhibit almost narcissistic tendencies, or at the very least massive egos.*

To make this happen, Lundmark embarked on a series of projects to reignite the innovation culture at Konecranes. He spoke openly about the company's blunders and where they were lacking. He voiced his own insecurities and how humbled he had been by observing the results of the industrial hackathons that the company ran. He signalled that he himself lacked much of the technical expertise required to realize innovation but also a desire to learn and to understand. Succinctly put, he was honest about his own shortcomings and made it very clear that he wanted to hear ideas from all parts of the organization, not just those he considered 'innovative'. By way of this honesty, he managed to form a far more responsive and engaged organization, particularly when it came to innovation, as people saw that the openness of the CEO signalled that they could speak up about their own ideas and their own take on things. For leaders, we might even talk of a responsibility of vulnerability, as a necessary aspect of innovation cultures. Where respect makes people feel safe and reciprocity supports ideas, a culture of responsibility allows for a far more honest conversation about ideas and innovation.

*Key takeaway: Deep innovation cultures value taking responsibility, be this through direct action or radical honesty.*

## Reflection

All three elements of deep innovation cultures mentioned earlier are things that cannot be embedded in a culture without the fourth, and most fickle, element, *reflection*. Shallow innovation thinking survives when it doesn't get challenged, when audiences just merrily nod along. This is for instance why innovation theatre has such a hold on us and why mediocre innovation consultants can still successfully ply their trade. As innovation fatigue reaches epidemic levels, we have become less and less adept at reflecting on what innovation means, how we

*Cultures of deep innovation do not just 'do innovation', but continuously challenge and question it.*

can compare different forms of innovation and what we should do when people start showing signs of innovation stress. Cultures of deep innovation do not just 'do innovation', but continuously challenge and question it. By doing so, they ensure that the organization keeps learning and developing, rather than getting caught up in shallow innovation games.

For a fine example of this, consider the work of Andoni Aduriz at his world-famous restaurant Mugaritz. A mainstay on lists of the greatest restaurants in the world, Mugaritz is a laboratory for culinary innovation. Here, Aduriz can explore both novel cooking techniques but also the very notion of *haute cuisine*. Some years ago, as I was interviewing him, he suddenly started talking with great passion about his ideas regarding 'cocina insípida', or insipid cooking. In effect, he was experimenting with entire meals that would lack flavour altogether, or at least have very little, with the experience primarily focusing on various textures and the feeling of eating. Whilst this might not sound terribly appetizing, it is a fine expression of the depth of Aduriz's innovation thinking. For what is innovation if not the re-evaluation of assumptions? Until the emergence of the sharing economy, we used to assume that you needed to own cars to run a taxi business or houses to serve accommodation. Until the emergence of streaming media, we assumed the music business was all about selling pieces of plastic (vinyl or polycarbonate). When Aduriz started asking questions about whether you could create cuisine without flavours, he was following a core innovation process, one where we look at our current knowledge and competence and start asking the really difficult questions about the same.

This might seem like a simple thing, but it is one of the most difficult ones there is. We humans are, as previously noted, not famous for our capacity for self-criticism, and when we do engage in such it far too often degenerates into self-flagellation, doubt and imposter syndrome. To do what Aduriz does, which is to find a balance between questioning your own assumptions/competencies and taking pride in developing from there, can take a lifetime to master. Things are not made any less complicated by trying to make reflection a core value in a culture, to extend a continuous process of challenging assumptions and looking beyond current competencies from a personal to an interpersonal plane. Still, this is what is needed for an organization to have a sustained culture of innovation, one that can transcend the innovations that are for the innovations to come.

## Embedding reflection: a guide for leaders

To make an organization reflective is a never-ending journey. To embed reflection into an organization is to make it constantly ask questions, always being prepared to learn and not shying away from leaving things behind. For a leader, this can be uncomfortable, as it means that the leader too can be questioned, but by instituting this deep into a culture one can build something that is stronger than the individual leader, something that can go on to innovate again and again. To do this, leaders need to consider how to:

*Celebrate questions and challenges.* Far too often, leaders try to downplay the challenges that an organization faces. To craft deep innovation cultures, leaders need to make difficult questions about the organization's competencies into something to revel in. Reward those who internally raise the most disturbing questions rather than those who ensure that all is well. Praise those who make others in the organization think.

*Incentivize intelligent self-doubt.* It is a given that people are uncomfortable with criticizing themselves and their shortcomings. We all wish to be seen as valuable members of our communities, so it is unlikely that employees will proactively offer up their self-doubts. Leaders thus need to have incentives in place for people to offer up their own inadequacies and to explore why what they used to know might not be what they need to know to go on and innovate. Leaders need to support and nurture such developments, ensuring that people feel safe to say when they no longer feel up to the task of innovation.

*Always test, always experiment.* An organization cannot reflect if it doesn't have things to reflect about. Also, if innovation is seen as utilizing things already tried out elsewhere, the organization will never progress from shallow innovation. Leaders need to ensure that the organization is constantly experimenting with new ideas and be very open to these experiments failing. Only by showing off a series of tests, including failed ones, will the culture of the organization be able to reflect about why some things succeed and others do not.

*Continue the dialogue.* Reflection never ends. Quite the opposite. Reflection is the faculty that ensures that we do not get stuck in old ideas, old ways of working, old perspectives on things – including things such as respect, reciprocity and responsibility. To craft an innovation culture for the long term, leaders need to realize that there is no finished state, no final form. Instead, there is a constant dialogue, where every new innovation is just an opening for new kinds of questions, new kinds of challenges. A success should be celebrated – for a while. But each success should then be questioned in turn and new experiments instituted.

## Daring to unlearn

If we look to organizations that have managed to stay innovative over a long time, organizations that have managed to reinvent themselves and find new paths for innovation, it can at times be quite difficult to pinpoint the exact innovation competencies they hold. This is because there may well have been no one, specific competency, but rather the meta-competency of being able to critique what has previously been understood as innovation in the company. Take IBM, for instance. A stalwart blue chip company, it has undergone several major shifts in its history, not to mention seen and produced many great innovations. In the early 1960s it transformed into an IT-only corporation, a shift that at the time was seen as foolhardy – after all, many considered IT to be just a fad. In the 1970s it introduced a plethora of great innovations, including relational databases, speech recognition and the floppy disc. In the 1980s it managed to use its brand and its technologies to remain a major player in IT, but it also started to lose its edge. IBM still innovates, but the size and costs of its corporate structure mean that it increasingly loses out to faster, nimbler companies. As a new era of computing dawns, defined by networked personal computers, IBM has created many of the technologies that define the era but fails to fully capture the value of these. When Louis Gerstner joined IBM as CEO in 1993, as the first outsider CEO since 1914, he started a process of radical questioning. Encouraging the company to question even the most fundamental aspects of itself, he started a process of renewal that was to become a thing of myth and legend.

Several previously central units were critically assessed and sold off – including the legendary printers and hard drives, previously seen as the very core of the business. New businesses, previously unthinkable, were first considered and then invested in heavily. IBM increasingly became a services company, delivering brand-agnostic solutions for corporations. Whilst retaining an edge in supercomputing and AI, many of the hardware units were sold off as IBM went into the new millennium, larger and more profitable than ever. But what was the innovation? It was less about what IBM did and more about what they no longer did. They dared to look at their business and what they'd been great at, reflected on whether that represented what they wanted to be in the future, and stopped doing the things that might have once represented innovation, but no longer did so. Was there resistance? Most certainly. But also a preparedness to think the unthinkable – an International Business Machines Corporation with far fewer business machines.

This, the capacity for *unlearning*, is a key component of productive reflection for deep innovation. The capacity for unlearning is one of the most difficult things to teach or to enact in a culture. We are primed to value learning by our parents and our teachers, and we've learnt something, we're primed to protect this. In an organization, this tendency is further enhanced. I at one time worked with a company that had a large business unit that worked with a specific kind of radio technology. They were very well versed in the ins and outs of this technology and had mastered the art of optimizing them. The problem? A different technology was becoming more and more popular, and the company had another business unit that was betting big on this. As the company quite openly nurtured a culture in which business units were encouraged to compete rather than collaborate (no silly reciprocities for them!), this caused 'my' unit no end of worry. What was remarkable, however, was the way they never faltered in their faith that the technology they knew would prevail in the end. Innovation meetings focused on trying to eke out even more development ideas based on the same technology, whilst other possible technologies were considered the enemy. As I suggested that one way to explore this new situation might be to think about a world in which their preferred technology simply wasn't used anymore, a visibly frustrated engineer blurted out: 'Oh, then what would be the point of even living?'

*The capacity for unlearning is a key component of productive reflection for deep innovation.*

## Innovation and emotional agility

What so often kills the innovation culture in an organization is, as previously noted, a tendency not to reflect on innovation and what it means to the organization, but instead to merely repeat platitudes about it. Such magical thinking, where one attempts to bring in innovation by way of invocation (look in a mirror and slowly say Steve Job's name three times...), often leads to exhaustion in the organization, not to mention an overall negativity towards similar attempts. In the end, the organization can well be suffused with an innovation pessimism. What is worse, leaders often revert to a strange kind of denialism, where the organization is in effect forbidden from giving voice to this pessimism – and instead is required to join in repeat performances of what brought it about in the first place.

In her fine book on handling complex emotions, *Emotional Agility: Get unstuck, embrace change and thrive in work and life*,[8] Susan David discusses the perils of such forced optimism and the folly of not being honest with our negative emotions. Instead, she argues, the best leaders, the most productive people, and those who have mastered work-life balance are united in that they all have found ways of using emotional agility. This is a process that emphasizes taking your emotions and emotional states seriously but also the capacity to analyse them in a detached fashion. Some might call it reflection.

In the context of innovation, this means that we (both as individuals and as cultures) need to learn to recognize the emotional patterns we create in relation to novelty, learning and change in organizations. If we continuously repeat demands for more innovation, but this doesn't lead to much, we need to do more than just increase the frequency of the demands. Instead, we need to be able to face our fears, our feelings of inadequacy, even our feelings of being bored by yet another call for innovation, and consider why these exist. On a cultural level, we need to allow for people to express their innovation fatigue, for it is only by giving words to existing negative emotions around innovation that we can start combatting it. Deep innovation cultures have an acceptance for there being negative emotions around innovation, and rather than ignore these, they lift them up as topics to discuss and reflect on.

As a cultural value, reflection allows for us to be mindful of our relationship with our history, our competencies, even our fears and insecurities. It is a necessary part of cultures that wish to develop and progress, for it is only through an ongoing engagement with the culture's own assumptions that an organization can keep renewing itself.

*Key takeaway: Deep innovation cultures celebrate unlearning and are prepared to reflect even on the negative and painful aspects of innovation.*

## Crafting innovation cultures

To craft an innovation culture is to move away from a mindset that emphasizes the management of ideas and projects, towards a mindset that looks more holistically at whether the culture is supporting and nurturing towards new ideas. Not uncritically so, but in a manner that emphasizes dialogue, engagement and challenges. I started by calling this 'thinking like a farmer', and I would like to return to this. A farmer understands that it isn't enough to just throw out some seed and wait for the crops to grow. No, you need to till the earth, ensure that seedlings are protected and, once the harvest is in, you need to start anew.

To ensure an innovation culture that truly captures cognitive surplus and engages everyone, you need psychological safety, you need respect and you need reciprocity. This to make people feel that innovation is meaningful and to make sure that they wish to take responsibility. Failure to do so, failure to institute psychological safety and fundamental civility might not create immediate, visible reactions in the culture. People may still take part in innovation theatre, but they will be disengaged and will no longer bring the kind of reflection that can deepen innovation engagements.

The reason I separate deep and shallow innovation is to highlight the fundamental differences at play here. A culture that only focuses on showy things and surface effects can look innovative, but it will not generate valuable, meaningful change in the long run. In order to build an innovation culture that creates unique and impactful things, you need a strong foundation of shared and lived values. With these in place, we can move towards expanding our idea-space – through imagination, curiosity and play. It is to this work we will turn in the next chapter.

# CHAPTER FOUR

# The imagination premium

*Pushing beyond fatigue, thinking beyond boundaries*

'*The imagination is a powerful agent for creating as it were a second nature out of the material supplied to it by actual nature.*' IMMANUEL KANT

## Building a better cornucopia

For an innovation culture to become a powerful creator of value, it needs ideas to nurture, develop and deepen. (Thank you, Captain Obvious!) On the one hand, this isn't a problem. A strong innovation culture will by its very nature be far better at picking up the ideas that naturally exist in an organization. As stated in the very first chapter of this book, there are no organizations that lack ideas, and a culture with a strong respect for ideas and a fundamental psychological safety will keep innovating. In this manner, organizations truly can be the gift that keeps giving. That said, organizations should also consider the processes that might temper this and how paying attention to matters such as curiosity and imagination can generate not just more ideas but better ideas. Stronger seedlings, if you will.

In Greek mythology, the cornucopia was a horn, more precisely the horn of plenty. It was a symbol for abundance and fertility, for nature's capacity to create and feed us. In the stories it became a magical object, so that it in one telling was the horn of the goat Amalthea that fed her milk to the infant Zeus (yes, really). Being a rambunctious baby, one day Zeus accidentally broke off one of the horns of said goat, which then magically became capable of providing unending amounts of food, as tends to happen when there's a baby god about.

As metaphors go, cornucopia is a fine one for organizational creativity. An organization, simply by force of having people working together and trying to solve problems, is a veritable horn of plenty of ideas. People cannot help themselves when it comes to having ideas, and although many of these will be killed or otherwise ignored, they're still there. Come tomorrow, there will be still more ideas around.

Yet, cornucopias can have their issues too. The original cornucopia was often portrayed as overflowing with fruit, honey and cereal. Which is fine, but once in a while you will get a yearning for tacos al pastor. In a similar way, your organization will almost certainly generate ideas, plenty of them, but over time these too can get in a rut. The same idea, or variations on the same, will pop up over and over again, and there might be fewer and fewer of those really off-the-wall ideas (particularly if they've not tended to be respected and reciprocated). So whilst working on the foundation of an innovation culture, we need also to look at how we can enhance the ideas generated in the organization – building a better cornucopia, if you will. To do this, we need to address the manner in which ideas are created. For many, this means 'working with creativity', with all the horrors this can bring in a corporate setting. The brainstorms and the Post-it® notes, the consultants and the away days – all elements well known to induce innovation fatigue. But behind such dreary creativity exercises lurks something wilder, something less likely to cause fatigue. *Dig deep enough, and you will find your organization's imagination.*

## Imagination: tricky, troubling and terrific

For the innovation industry, nothing is more attractive than the crystal-clear process, the one that can easily be turned into an innovation book or a model for innovation consultancy. This dream of a step-by-step, painting-by-numbers model for innovation is further shared by many a business leader, who would wish for nothing more than a surefire way to innovate. The problem, however, lies in the fact that true innovation comes down to matters that cannot be flowcharted. There's no checklist for respect. Creativity can't be captured in a 2×2 matrix, because it doesn't fit frameworks so much as breaks them. What leaders who wish for deep innovation in their organizations must do is to accept this fundamental uncertainty. They need to accept that sometimes it has to be pure unadulterated human imagination, the most unmanageable dynamic of all, that calls the shots.

Imagination, often overlooked in innovation literature as childish and non-serious, is a power that is difficult to define. It might be described as our mind's unfettered potential for thinking up new ideas, concepts and images, or as the faculty through which our mind can think the previously unthinkable. To some, imagination is the less practical part of creativity. This is when we call something an innovation if it works and can be sold (in one way or another), and we call something creative if it at least *could* work. Imagination has no such boundaries. Imagination can dream up solutions that are utterly ridiculous, such as the replicators in *Star Trek* that could make any food you wished for appear instantaneously, or the magical objects in *Harry Potter*.

Through this association with the impossible and the incredible, imagination has a sullied reputation in the world of business. Whilst it might be appreciated in speeches and promotional materials, it is often denigrated in practice. In my own work, I can no longer count the number of times a manager has asked that ideas be 'realistic' or 'practical' when we do an ideas session, nor the number of times a CEO has urged people not to go 'too crazy'. As a word, if brought up in a session with a board of directors, imagination tends to elicit grimaces rather than enthusiasm, and more than once I've had to contend with the claim that only academics could be so far removed from the practice of business as to suggest imagination is something worthy of attention.

Yet almost every great innovation we have has at one point been a tremendous leap of imagination! Most great innovations have required considerable imagination, be it flight, travelling at speeds over 100 km/h, being able to speak to people on the other side of the planet, or simply the possibility of being able to book a place on the sofa of a complete stranger from the comfort of your magic slab of glass. Before innovations are realized, they are simply... figments of our imagination.

*Almost every great innovation we have has at one point been a tremendous leap of imagination!*

## Good engineers/bad engineers

Once upon a time the Finnish company Nokia was a behemoth, a world-defining communication and mobile technology company that seemingly could do no wrong. It was technologically astute, obsessive about operational efficiency and hired some of the smartest people on the planet – and a fair few who might not have been but were convinced they were. They were Masters of the (Mobile Phone) Universe, and they knew it. They also created some of the finest products the world had ever seen, including the 3110 that still to this day is spoken about in reverential tones. For many, not least within Nokia, their sudden fall from grace was shocking, and even though the company has managed to find new success by focusing on network technologies, their waning fortunes are a good illustration of what happens when a company's creative culture decays.

Nokia was always a company by engineers, for engineers. It was a marvel of operational efficiency and very much in the thrall of best practices (or, as I like to call them, 'sh-t that used to...' Oh. I already used that one, didn't I?). It hired many exceptionally talented people and established a culture that emphasized performance and excellence – neither of which is bad in and of itself. It also developed a reputation of being tough negotiators, always demanding more. Amidst all of this, it also invested heavily in innovation and did allow for a number of imaginative projects. Their top management team worked closely with a colourful media philosopher, and the company had some of the world's finest behavioural researchers and designers on their payroll (such as the almost supernaturally talented Jan Chipchase). In addition, the R&D wing of Nokia developed very advanced concepts and technologies, including one of the first prototypes of the 'slab of glass' that became the modern smartphone (and seen as the quintessential icon of Apple's innovation dominance).

So why, then, did everything go so very wrong? Why, when the company seemed to hold all the aces (innovative projects, talented staff, robust market power, not to mention access to astronomical amounts of money), did they miss out on the rise of the modern smartphone and the next stage of how consumers approached mobile communications? It wasn't because they lacked analytical skill, or smarts, or even general innovativeness. It was simply because as a culture, they couldn't see beyond the things that had brought them their historical success, the things beyond. They knew their best practices, they felt they knew 'what worked'. They had the data, and they couldn't see beyond it. For data is not all. In fact, for all the hype around it, too much focus on the data can cripple a corporation.

## Business in the imagination age

Imagine the following: an age in which Google, Amazon, IBM and a fair few Chinese companies are competing on who can sell you cheap, plug-and-play AIs, capable of crunching your data in ways you can hardly imagi… consider at the current time. An age in which big data is as cheap as electricity. An age in which rigorous data analytics is as widespread as Excel. It is coming, and it might be here quicker than you realize. In such an age, is an AI a competitive advantage? No, of course it isn't. It's about as much a competitive advantage as having internet access in your office. Is data analytics? Only insofar as it is a must-have, a little like cash flow management. That said, just because you have great insight into your historical management of cash reserves doesn't mean that you have any insight into how they need to be used in the future. Lest we forget, Blockbuster Video had an *amazing* amount of data about what movies people rented from the store, back when people rented videos from the store. At their peak, Blockbuster had more than 9,000 such stores and the best practices around. At the moment of writing, there's one left. It's in Bend, the seventh most populous city in Oregon, and it has become something of a tourist destination.

Today, many companies believe that investments in digital tools will protect them, when the reality is that these investments are merely the price you pay to play today. Yet in an age of cheap digital analytics and AI everywhere, imagination isn't going anywhere. On the contrary. As the competitive advantage of data shrinks, imagination is where the money is. This is of course not an original observation, and a number of people (not to mention organizations such as OECD) have identified how central imagination will be in tomorrow's business. The term 'imagination age' as the age that will supersede the Information Age was first suggested by Charlie Magee in 1993,[1] but used by several people since. The exact phrasing, however, is less important than the key insight. The Industrial Age was a story about how electricity went from being a curiosity to something omnipresent, about how manufacturing developed so that commodities became almost unimaginably cheap, and how advanced logistics made same-day deliveries and avocados in winter not just possible, but normal. Now, part of this overlapped with the Information Age, and not all of it was without issues (or ecological costs), but still. The Information Age has been a story about communication becoming instantaneous, about supercomputers becoming things we casually carry one or two of with us at all times (or if you're like me, three), as well as any and every kind of data processing and storage becoming ever cheaper, to the point where it is conceivable they will one day be practically free (at least until we factor in energy costs).

*As the competitive advantage of data shrinks, imagination is where the money is.*

Amidst this radical drop in a multitude of costs, there is one constant. Someone needs to think of what to produce, what to ship, what to analyse. The internet without content is a delightful invention but of interest mainly to those who get excited about data architectures. All the factories of Shenzhen would stand still if there was no-one around dreaming up the gadgets, gizmos and gewgaws they produce today. As industry and manufacturing become ever cheaper, imagination becomes more important. Right now we're seeing the next cycle of it, for as digitalization (of all kinds, including AI) becomes ever cheaper and easier to use, imagination becomes more valuable still. As muscle is needed for less and less in business, and processing data and running through routines and best practices can soon be handed over to algorithmic entities, then the only real competitive advantage will be the capacity to think beyond the data. To do what Nokia didn't. To see what others can't. To, in a word, imagine (cue Lennon, circa 1971...). Welcome to the Imagination Age.

## The imagination premium

Now, this is of course not always as straightforward as all that, and as e.g. Rita McGrath has noted, imagination is also something that is interpreted and can be ascribed to you, wrongly or rightly. Together with her collaborators, she has written about 'the imagination premium',[2] which in her use refers to how the stock market can create expectations regarding your capacity for sustainable imagination. For instance, much of Amazon's stock market value has been driven by an expectation that the house that Bezos built can keep up their tradition of finding imaginative ways of hooking customers and delivering value. But just because investors are at times prepared to pay a big premium for the perceived capacity for imagination in a company, doesn't mean that this guarantees said imagination. Lest we forget, Enron – the energy, commodity and services company from Texas – was at one point seen as a veritable powerhouse of imagination. They seemed always capable of eking profits out of seemingly impossible positions and were by *Fortune* crowned 'America's Most Innovative Company' six years in a row (1995–2000). Sadly, their imagination was primarily focused on highly creative forms of accounting and outright fraud, which brought the company tumbling down in 2001. As it turned out, much of the vaunted value of Enron was built on little more than hopes and impossible dreams, and as the extent of the deception became apparent, Enron went bankrupt in one of the biggest corporate scandals of all time.

To some, this might seem like a blow against imagination. Why not just stick to what you know and not get mired in things that can be used for both good and evil? I would contend it is *specifically* because of this that we need to think long and hard about imagination in our organizations. We also need to stop imagining that routines, creativity and imagination are wholly separate faculties.

This is because there is a big mistake that we often make when thinking about human cognition and thought. As we are trained to think in parts rather than wholes, we often envision thinking as something done through individual, separate faculties. We see memory and remembering as one thing, doing maths and logics as another, thinking creatively as a third. This is wrong, just like the old wives' tales about separate parts of the brain doing separate things. Just like in all thinking, the brain might activate one part more than others when, for instance, trying to remember the name of an old acquaintance, but this does not mean that the other parts are wholly disengaged. Much like an organization works effectively when everyone is engaged to at least some minimum level, thinking works by connections and networked effects. Things like creativity and imagination are thus not faculties wholly separate from other forms of thinking, but rather very much dependent on the same.

This is the real imagination premium. It represents what we can achieve when we understand the full power of the human mind, and beyond even this, the true power that can be harnessed when this isn't just wasted with fatiguing meetings and pointless exercises, but respected and nurtured. An organization with 1,000 employees has 1,000 engines of imagination to utilize, yet it often connects with only a handful of these. What would you do to a CEO that only has his or her employees work for 10 minutes out of every 8 hours? Fire them, of course, as they are being inefficient beyond measure. Yet I have seen companies that utilize the imagination of 20 in 1,000 people, and this is seemingly OK. The ratios are the same, and the 98 per cent of unused imagination is a premium worth thinking long and hard (and deep) about.

## Thinking, fast and slow and deep

To understand imagination, then, is not to make out how a closed mode of thinking works, but rather to grasp how layered human thought is. Daniel Kahneman famously, in his bestselling *Thinking, Fast and Slow*[3] delineated a System 1 and a System 2 for thinking. The former is fast, based on instincts and immediate responses, whilst the latter is more deliberate and logical. One way to think about imagination is to start from here but then to go considerably deeper. I like to picture this as a digging down, going from the easily shifted topsoil of our instinctive mind, all the way down to the hard-to-reach sedimentary rock of imagination. This is so as to turn our usual perception of imagination as fluffy and easy on its head – not least because for organizations, imagination can often be the hardest thing of all. Just ask Blockbuster.

Most thinking, in organizations and amongst individuals, is organized by **routines**, learnt patterns and behaviours that have worked decently well before and which people as a consequence often resort to even when faced with a new problem. This is the kind of thinking that is easiest for us to turn to, as we can just use preprogrammed heuristics. If morning, get coffee. Socks before shoes. If a customer complains, blame the IT system. This kind of thinking is very important, as it helps us get through the day and handle well-known and well-understood situations. We use this mode of thinking so often and so without reflection that we don't even necessarily see how this might also lead to problems. This is Kahneman's System 1 thinking, and just as he details, it can bring in a plethora of biases, where our shortcuts and heuristics can make us act in quite irrational ways. Still, it is important to note that this is always (always!) our brain's go-to system for dealing with issues. No matter whether it is a new problem to be solved or ideas to be brainstormed, the first things out of our system of thinking will be routine solutions – the easiest, most comfortable ideas we can think of.

When faced with more complex problems, we start engaging what Kahneman would call System 2. This is a more analytic mode of thinking, one that tries to combat the biases of the instinctive System 1. We might call this the level of *logic*, where we strive to stick to rules of thinking we already know but in a more conscious and considered manner. Here, we assess the data we have, think through the various processes we've previously tested for dealing with the problem, and pick the one we feel will be most suited to the task. As we're normally equipped with quite a few thinking tools, this kind of logical pick-and-mix comes naturally to us. Analytics, however, also suffers from a specific limitation. Logic is good for dealing with things that are relatively well known, or at least reminiscent of earlier problems. IF this, THEN that, assuming both this and that are known. This is the level of problem solving where there are clear answers to each issue, where best practices (no, I'm not doing **that** again) actually work. But sooner or later, every person and every organization will face a situation that isn't covered by previous knowledge, learnt processes and given solutions.

## Experimenting beyond logic

When we eke away from logic, or System 2 thinking, we usually do this in a tentative, exploratory manner. This is the level of *experiments*. Much discussed in contemporary management thinking, yet tragically ill understood, experiments represent a space in between logic and creativity. They are tests, things that may have been suggested by logic and previous experience, but they also contain an element of creativity, utilizing hypotheticals. For both organizations and individuals, this represents moving away from best practices and existing competencies, but doing so in a manner that explicitly delimits this. Experiments are interesting as they represent a knowing move away from the traditional sphere of thinking by introducing uncertainty and risk.

Going further still, we operate on a level of creativity, one where we move decidedly away from System 1 thinking but also start to bid *adieu* to System 2 thinking. Creativity, often defined as combining things that weren't previously combined, is a process in which we attempt to think beyond the logics we've been used to. What is important to note here, however, is that creativity isn't just some free space of thinking, a gear we can easily connect to. On the contrary, our creativity is often influenced and framed by our routine, logical way of looking at the world. Thus, if you are an engineer, your creative 'toolkit' will contain many routines and logics of engineering. You will also be more likely to see creativity in engineering solutions and less likely to appreciate forms of creativity that spring from other kinds of experience and knowledge.

This also affects organizations. An organization like Nokia will have a number of established routines and logics that always frame what is considered creative and what isn't. For a technology company, this can mean a profound inability to see any value in experimenting with new kinds of service offerings, whereas it may well appreciate creative new technical solutions – at least in the kind of technology they are comfortable with.

*Creativity, as it is understood by an individual or an organization, isn't necessarily all that creative.*

Creativity, as it is understood by an individual or an organization, isn't necessarily all that creative. Engaging in experiments does not immediately ensure that the organization has a healthy creative culture, as it may well only be experimenting with things that are seen to be 'proper' and acceptable in the organization's culture. This is not to disparage experimentation but to emphasize that we need to understand the context within which things like experiments and creativity emerge. For even creativity can be done inside or outside the comfort zone.

## On the comfort zone

When speaking on creativity, from time to time I have to engage with the notion of comfort zones. It is an oft-used concept, although one we usually ascribe to others. We are quick to point out that others stick to their comfort zone, but we rarely address how much of our life we spend in one. In fact, we sometimes pay good money to enhance our zone of comfort – and conferences are great examples of this.

Think about it. What could possibly be a better example of the comfort zone than a conference? When at a conference, almost everything that can annoy a person in their everyday work is removed – the bosses, the colleagues and, maybe most importantly of all, the customers. At a conference we tend to be surrounded by like-minded people who are highly likely to have similar experiences and similar worries. Conferences can be wonderful places for challenging people's thinking and giving them a plethora of new ideas, but they can also be exceptionally powerful engines of creating bandwagon effects, supporting consensus and amplifying confirmation bias.

The same principles that make this true for conferences go for organizations as well, including but not limited to their internal dynamics. At least in organizations that primarily work in one sector, competencies are pooled but at the same time start narrowing the perspective of the organization. The members of the organization become comfortable with their acquired skill-sets and further start gravitating towards people in the organization who are most reminiscent of them. In many of the organizations I've worked with it is not seen as strange in the least that engineers routinely eat lunch with other engineers, or that key account managers mainly talk to other key account managers (often to complain about their customers). And why not? Even the way we often organize our companies follows this pattern, with separate sections for marketing, operations and so on. This is why some forward looking companies, such as

The Lego Group, emphasize what is known as T-shaped skills – having a broad, cross-function understanding of the business combined with a deep knowledge in a specialization.

For organizations wrestling with how to enhance creativity, the inherent tendency to remain in a comfort zone can be a tricky one to address. It doesn't necessarily show itself as an unwillingness to be creative, and I've often come across companies who are quite vocal about their love of creativity. As an example, I worked with a professional services company that simply could not understand why they were being out-innovated by nimbler competitors. As I audited them, the reason soon showed itself. Yes, the company had invested in innovation programmes and creative workshops, but all of these followed the exact same pattern. Ideas that were not in line with what the organization perceived as its core skillset were shot down, whereas ideas that started from the assumption that said skillsets were valuable and correct were lauded. The 'experiments' they had so enthusiastically described to me turned out to be impossible for a non-expert to separate from their 'business as usual'. It wasn't that they weren't trying, it was just that all the creativity they dared to engage with was coaxed and curtailed by logics they simply did not dare let go of. They needed to play more.

## Play like there's no-one watching

The corporate world has a complicated relationship with play – just like it has a complicated relationship with creativity and innovation. Yes, there is much lip service given to the importance of play, in some form or another, but this is seldom followed up with a true openness for allowing people to play at work. For all of our stated love of creativity, play still seems too childish and non-serious to be taken seriously in most companies. This is a shame, as play is one of the key ways in which we can break creativity's dependency on old logics.

Play is difficult, if not impossible to define, but for our purposes here, play might be defined as an exploratory activity that follows only its own, internal logic. This is to say that to play is to accept that usual rules do not apply, only the boundaries set by the playing itself. Thus, if we play pirates with our children, the sofa is a ship, the floor is water and that's just the way it is. This is not to say that play is unserious. Internal rules must be adhered to, and as anyone who has engaged in cosplay or live action role-playing can attest to, play can become very serious indeed.

In our current context, play might be best described as free experimentation. Whereas corporate experiments are often, problematically enough, limited by adhering too closely to forms of thinking that are already prevalent in the organization, play is a knowing break with what is already known and practised. Play is Tesla selling flamethrowers, or Burger King's original and free-wheeling Subservient Chicken-campaign (see www.subservientchicken.com/). Play is Chance the Rapper winning a Grammy without ever having signed a record contract and giving away all his music for free – his winning album *Coloring Book* was released on streaming services with no promotion.

That said, or precisely due to this, play is often difficult to engage with in an organization. In my work with the professional services firm I mentioned earlier in this chapter, I ran a workshop that encouraged participants to play-act as if the services they currently offered had been made illegal. The task I set was that they had quickly to create an offering they could attempt to sell to their current customers in place of the one I'd declared illegal. It was immediately clear that most people found the very premise of the workshop silly, even pointless. The services they offered, mainly related to finance, were not likely to be made illegal any time soon (although people might have had opinions regarding some of their more creative services with regards to taxes), and the more senior participants in particular were visibly uncomfortable with my suggestions for play.

What transpired, however, was a revelation. Some of the participants, seemingly thinking that they might just as well go for it, started play-acting some highly imaginative ideas. One was a notion that involved a high degree of co-creation, another imagined monetizing a support skillset the company had but rarely paid any attention to. In the play meetings, where some acted as customers, surprisingly effective methods for new business opportunities emerged. In our later debrief, several of the participants expressed joy over being able to freely suggest even wild ideas, unencumbered by what the company usually did and focused on.

*Play-acting and make-believe might seem less than serious, but what it in reality acts as is a portal to truly free, deep creativity – unfettered imagination.*

## The big I

If there is one thing I truly enjoy when talking about and teaching innovation to corporate boards, it is the sheer mischief of introducing 'imagination' into their vocabularies. I can sense that when I am brought in to give a talk or run a workshop, they assume I'll come and be very masculine and serious (I am, after all, a male professor with a beard), talking about masculine and serious things like 'innovation' and 'strategy' and 'leadership'. When I then start talking about imagination and the power of unfettered thinking, I can often see several of the directors recoil. Particularly at the introduction of the word imagination, which in their minds clearly is a 'girly' word, more suitable for the kindergarten than the boardroom.

It often takes quite a lot of convincing to communicate that imagination isn't all fun and games, but actually a deadly serious thing. Imagination is the very heart of creativity, the human faculty that allows us to think in an unfettered manner, free from limitations of education and experience, competence and collected truths. It is what we can reach when we go beyond

System 1 and System 2 thinking, beyond even creativity. It is here that thinking can be dark and daring, and ideas can truly be free. Getting to this level is difficult for humans, as we often shy away from this level of free, creative thinking. It is yet more difficult in organizations, where delving this deep can be actively discouraged.

But we need to respect imagination, as it is only through imagination that we can access the kind of ideas our routine processes automatically ignore and that our frames of logic and reference try to block for us. Yes, it is always the imaginative ideas that people try to kill first, and once innovation fatigue has set in, you're not necessarily even interested in accessing this level of thinking. Yet it is this we need to set free in order to go deep with creativity.

## Mining the imagination

What is important in this is to realize how imagination works, in individuals and in organizations. I like to think of it as a digging down, one that gets more difficult the deeper down you get. I use this metaphor to turn around the usual ways of presenting creativity, ones where our thinking ascends to higher and higher planes. This sort of romanticization can be quite dangerous, as it doesn't show how freeing your creative thinking actually involves working against other, more foundational forms. So rather than imagining scaling a summit, think of the human mind as a mine you dig,[4] as per Figure 4.1.

The first level, *routines*, represents a kind of topsoil of thinking. Easily accessed, we immediately have these at hand. We do not need to work for this, it is simply just there. This represents the first ideas we get, the most usual solutions – often straight from the gut – we deploy. Somewhat below this is a level of *logic*. This takes a little bit of work to get to, but we can all dig just below the topsoil. Sure, this is a little harder, and the soil

FIGURE 4.1   The many levels of (creative) thinking

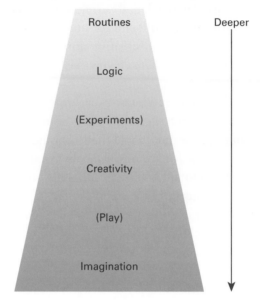

starts resisting a little, but as we are used to this work we rarely shy away from it (although it's not our first thing to do either).

*Experiments* represents things getting harder. A lot harder. They can be shallow or deep and show how we either put in serious work to access our creativity – think mineshafts of different depths – or just pretend that we do. In organizations, it is remarkable how often experiments are attempted but then abandoned just as quickly if they demand more work. This is because many experiments in organizations are very shallow and were never really meant to get very creative. They're show experiments. Once they're done, people think they never need to be re-attempted.

The layer that really interests us is of course the next one down, *creativity* itself. This should be thought of as a particularly deep section, one in which the top layers may be almost indistinguishable from logic but where we can drill down deeper and deeper, even starting to distance ourselves from routines and logic. Have you ever wondered how very traditional managers can speak so highly of creativity? This is because they've experienced the top layers and found them comforting enough, but they have never wanted to put in the work to drill down to where things start to be a bit dark and dangerous.

You might be curious as to why I placed *play* at such a deep level, which would seem to indicate that it is difficult. Surely play is anything *but* difficult? You would think that, but you would be wrong. For most adults, play is very difficult indeed. In organizations it can be nigh impossible. This is because play is only superficially easy. Yes, anyone can play for a minute or two. Playing a computer game is easy, because you often do it in isolation and with the full support of the game. Playing for an extended period, in a real-life setting, is something entirely different. This is because playing of the kind I'm referencing here requires that you are able not only to leave behind the frameworks and logics that have defined your entire working life, not to mention the working life of all those you're playing with, but to do so in a sustained fashion. We find it difficult because it untethers us, but also because we feel vulnerable, even silly whilst doing so. Yet we must, if we are to break through to the final level.

*For most adults, play is very difficult indeed. In organizations it can be nigh impossible.*

This, unsurprisingly, is the level of *imagination*. This is the level that requires the greatest amount of work to connect with, a bedrock of thinking that can only be accessed by consciously distancing oneself from that which is normally thought of as reason and logic. Going this deep can cause great unease in corporations, as we are well and truly away from processes as usual. Still it is at this depth that truly disruptive ideas can emerge, and one of the reasons why startups often have an easier time connecting with this is because they do not carry the same kind of intellectual baggage.

So, in order to benefit from the imagination premium, and in order to use imagination to kill innovation fatigue, we need to reconnect with a very deep level of thinking. To help with this, organizations need diversity, which we'll address in the next chapter, and courage, which we'll look at in the antepenultimate[5] chapter. For now, we still have time to look at one critical tool in innovation mining, which is also a key part of deep creativity – curiosity.

## Curiosity: it never killed the cat

As children, we are sometimes cautioned not to be too curious. Sometimes this is because parents might not wish for kids to find stashed-away presents; but more often it is because curiosity is seen as a dangerous thing. We are told not to explore too much and that testing things out can get you killed. As children are curious by nature, we often don't listen, and as teens we gleefully ignore warnings, curious about all that the world has to offer. Over time, though, we become less and less curious.

Something similar happens in organizations. Startups and other young organizations are often happy to test things, to, in the words of Facebook, 'move fast and break things'. Over time, however, organizations age much like the rest of us. As they mature, they become less and less curious about the world (and even Facebook has retired their old motto). As companies become increasingly caught up in the clients they know, the competencies they're comfortable with, and their own way of viewing the world (or reducing it to simple KPIs), they increasingly build themselves a filter bubble that keeps out novel information and the imagination this might spark. If we look to the history of great business failures – be it Kodak, Blockbuster, or Toys 'R' Us – these often follow a

*So how do you make sure that your organization remains curious?*

depressingly common pattern. It's never that the company lacked acumen, or people with ideas, or the resources to try out new things. Neither does business failure in the face of new technologies or new consumer behaviours stem from change being so quick that it is impossible to react to it. No, in almost all cases the writing was on the wall for some time, but too few in the company cared enough to read it. They simply weren't all that interested. So how do you make sure that your organization remains curious?

Roche (or if you like the full name, F. Hoffmann-La Roche AG) is a major pharmaceutical company founded in 1896. Despite being in a highly competitive industry, and one where investments into innovation can be punishingly expensive, Roche has been incredibly successful. In 2017, they increased their dividend for the 31st consecutive year and had sales of US $53.5 billion. There are of course many reasons for such success, such as a Swiss attention to detail and well-executed strategies, but one core component has always been their culture of independent research and a commitment to curiosity. As an example, consider the following fact, communicated to me by a vice president from their diagnostics field. In the specialization we were discussing, there are two major R&D centres within the Roche Group. This in and of itself is not interesting at all. The interesting thing is that as a matter of policy, the two research centres were firewalled, i.e. there was to be no communication between them, effectively making them competitors. Whilst this might seem like a strange thing to want, the logic is in fact quite brilliant. As the researchers in these two centres could never be sure what their counterparts were doing, both centres showcased a high degree of curiosity when it came to keeping up with medical science, communicating with people outside the organization and taking part in odd and obscure conferences and workshops. As neither unit could be entirely sure they weren't falling behind or missing out, their curiosity was not so much piqued as turbo-charged.

## A curiosity crisis (and escaping it)

Although we need to be careful about drawing conclusions from single cases, Roche's story still contains a number of key points when it comes to curiosity and how it can be enhanced within an organization. But before we move on to this, let us look at some of the costs of not being curious enough. One of the great curiosity researchers in the world is a behavioural scientist by the name of Francesca Gino. Writing in *Harvard Business Review*,[6] she disclosed the results of a major study on curiosity in the workplace. Shockingly, her study showed that only 24 per cent (so less than one person in four) reported regularly feeling curious at work. Even more scary was that 70 per cent reported that their organizations had barriers that hindered them from asking questions – and thus to develop the business. This is well in line with other similar studies and highlights an odd paradox in today's organizations: **People are told to be innovative, but discouraged from asking questions and being curious.**

Such a curiosity crisis can of course spell doom for an organization, and Gino goes on to recommend hiring people who are naturally curious, emphasizing learning and leading by example to overcome this. Whilst this is certainly good advice, I have personally found that just like imagination needs to be mined, curiosity needs to be actively encouraged. This means that it isn't enough to merely wish for a more curious workforce but to take active and impactful steps to ensure curiosity. Just like imagination, curiosity may come naturally to children, but this doesn't mean it is easy to rekindle in adults. In my own work, three specific themes have emerged in relation to this, and in all three cases, a strong link between curiosity and imagination is clearly present.

The first is related to how people find things to be curious about. In several projects I've done, I've insisted on *conducting a comprehensive review of a company's idea inputs*. Whilst noting that an organization needs fresh inputs to generate imaginative ideas might seem self-evident and trivial, the fact is that most organizations have little to no strategic understanding of what is read, studied, followed and explored within them. In my experience, four out of five organizations have little to no systematic attempts to bring in a broad range of different and diverse inputs into their organizations. Rather, the typical case is that new inputs are mostly collected from the general business media (that all the competitors follow as well), industry media (ditto) and industry conferences (even more ditto). With a majority of inputs thus being well known to all the usual actors, and no plan in place for harvesting inputs and insights from more diverse sources, the organization might well have a *desire* for curiosity without the requisite framework to make this desire usable. An action point here would then be to create systems for harvesting new insights, which can range from complex idea management systems to something as simple as paying attention to which magazines are read in the organization. Again, in an organization, innovation capabilities might hinge on the smallest things.

The second theme has to do with ***incentivizing exploration***. Most companies only have real incentives for things such as meeting pre-set sales targets or similar KPIs. Peculiarly enough, this means that employees and managers focus primarily on said targets and indicators, at the expense of curiosity and exploration. In a conversation with a top executive in the marine industry, who was very worried about the low levels of innovation in his company when compared to the competition, I suggested that he simply change incentive structures so that bonuses would only be paid out if managers could show that they'd explored a number of hitherto untested ideas and possibilities. The executive replied that this would be highly irresponsible, as his managers could then be 'rewarded for doing unnecessary things'. This was not a fool, but a top executive who had been so brainwashed by the innovation industry that he truly believed that innovation could be achieved without 'unnecessary' exploration. Still, if we pay people to stick to what they know and punish them for curiosity, we cannot at the same time be surprised if they are less than engaged with creativity and innovation.

The third theme of this is ***disincentivizing comfort and safety***. Incentives are important, but we shouldn't just look to positive such. Negative incentives, also known as 'punishments', might sound like tools of oppressive management and the kind of harsh paternalism that can create a toxic workplace culture. Still, we need to think not only about how to reward curiosity but also how to ensure that people have an incentive not to remain in their comfort zone. As an example, Intel has for a long time used job rotation as a strategic tool through which people fill in temporary positions and learn new technologies. As companies become more and more dependent on developing their imagination potential, such processes will move from being quirky aberrations to necessary ways to keep people curious. It used to be that you never got fired for buying IBM, but in the future the opposite might be true...

## Getting serious about imagination

The key message of this chapter is that imagination only looks like a childish, less than serious thing. For companies wanting to succeed in the Imagination Age, few things could be more serious. Companies will need to move away from shallow experiments, get busy playing and working with their curiosity. However, in order to do this, leaders need to do more than merely wish for imaginative organizations.

What is needed, instead, are leaders who encourage employees to get 'crazy', who dare to think beyond logic and who push for challenging, difficult-to-stomach experiments. Leaders who, like the earlier mentioned Andoni Aduriz, push their organizations far outside their comfort zone – even when doing so might make some people doubt their sanity.

They need to work on their innovation cultures but also build organizations that optimize for imagination and have the courage and ambition to do the hard work that imagination demands. It is to these issues we will now turn.

# CHAPTER FIVE

# Innovative by design

## Diversity and the trouble with monocultures

*'Everybody believes in innovation until they see it. Then they think, "Oh, no; that'll never work. It's too different".'*
NOLAN BUSHNELL

## Macho madness

Let's be frank: innovation thinking suffers from a troubling machismo. From Menlo Park to Microsoft, innovation has often been assumed to be a man's world, and whilst companies have learnt to pay lip service to diversity, this doesn't always extend to the hallowed work of innovation. Emily Chang has detailed this in her excellent if troubling *Brotopia: Breaking up the boys' club of Silicon Valley,*[1] showing that there is often a distinct gender bias in the ways we think about and portray innovation and innovative organizations. Clichés regarding what constitutes a real coder or an innovative genius still persist, and we are still more likely to refer to Steve Jobs than Hedy Lamarr when discussing innovators. Ms. Lamarr may have originated technologies that made things such as Bluetooth and WiFi possible,[2] but we're still more likely go to the iconic image of Jobs in his black turtleneck when we need a quick icon for innovation.

In school, we're taught that Edison gave us the lightbulb and that the telephone was invented by Alexander Graham Bell (both are dubious simplifications, but let's not get caught up in that), but not that Josephine Cochrane invented the first commercially successful dishwasher (in 1886). If you ask people to name the woman who created the first treatment for leukaemia, the first immune-suppressive agent (used to massively increase the success rate of organ transplants), the first successful drug for treating herpes, and who even had a hand in the creation of AZT, the first medication to treat and even prevent HIV/AIDS, they will in all likelihood question that such a person ever even existed. If one woman had done all that, surely she'd be world famous? Well, one woman did. Her name was Gertrude Belle Elion, and although she never even got a formal PhD, she went on to win the Nobel Prize in Physiology or Medicine in 1988 (shared with George Hitchings and James Black). She is of course well known in the field of medicine, particularly amongst those with an interest in biochemistry, but to most she is utterly unknown, even though she in addition to the impressive list above also created medicines for things such as gout, malaria and meningitis. In short, she literally cured some cancers and has saved untold people from death. Now, imagine a man had done all that. Would he, too, be almost unknown? Doubtful. Very doubtful. Particularly as men have a tendency to become world famous for much, much less.

*Put somewhat differently, innovation has a diversity problem.* It is not because diversity and innovation are at odds with each other; quite the contrary. Innovation thrives on diversity, to the point where we might say that diversity is one of the most important driving forces thereof. But this simple fact, proven time and time again,[3] still struggles to change the macho logic, vernacular and attitudes in much of both innovation literature and innovation initiatives in organizations.

This is something I see time and time again in my work. I join innovation workshops, only to find that they are led by young, Caucasian men, even in countries where these represent a minority. I meet Chief Innovation Officers

*Innovation has a diversity problem.*

and, unsurprisingly, they look like the older (male) relatives of the men in the preceding sentence. I join panels on innovation, only to find that they consist solely of people who look very much like I do. And yes, I can see the irony in bringing this up as a white, Caucasian man, who is by now solidly middle class (although not too far removed from my rural and working-class roots). I may be an innovation professor, but I have to admit that I look the part. Which is part of the problem.

## Innovation and privilege

It is rarely a comfortable conversation, but it is one we need to have: ***there is an element of privilege to innovation.*** Regardless of whether we're talking about an individual or an organization, it is easier to try out new things if you do not need to fight for your subsistence. As a self-evident example, at least everywhere except in the innovation industry, being dirt poor and thus unable to afford higher education will put up barriers for your propensity to innovate. Sure, a lot of the great innovators were drop-outs, but the reason they dropped out of university was rarely that they couldn't afford to study but rather that they could afford to try out other things. In many cases they had safety nets, not to mention networks to draw on. Even in cases where such innovators emerge out of more humble backgrounds, everything is relative.

Take Steve Jobs. His (adoptive) parents were blue collar workers and not very well off, but they were highly supportive to the point where they spent their life savings in order to move to a better school district. Later on, they spent more still to pay for Job's studies at the decidedly expensive Reed College (that he dropped out of). Whilst this doesn't mean Jobs came from money, it should also be noted that not all rebellious children have parents that can buy houses, even if modest ones, in order to ensure a more suitable school for their child. Neither does every talented but unfocused child have parents that can send them to a university to drop out of. In addition to being talented and driven, Jobs was also lucky. He was at the right place at the right time and, even more importantly, he fitted in. He was good-looking, had spent much of his childhood around engineers and seems to have had a relaxed attitude to experimenting with drugs,[4] the kind that often comes from knowing that the police don't target your kind. Yes, he sold his minibus in order to get funding for Apple, but it should be noted that he had a minibus to start with. Did any of this guarantee anything? Of course not. Neither does it take away from his drive or vision or achievements. But it is there, and it is there more for some than others.

We can see something similar on an organizational level. In the innovation literature there has long been a debate about whether big organizations or small ones are better at innovation. The popular answer, based more in popular culture and media depictions than in actual data, is that small organizations can out-innovate bigger rivals, as the latter are seen as stodgy, traditional and bureaucratic. This assumption has driven much of the writing on disruptive innovation, as well as inspiring a gazillion or so startup founders with big dreams and scant resources. It is the story we want to hear, one where you need only grit and perseverance to kill the lumbering dinosaurs of the corporate world. But like many of the stories we love, it doesn't quite live up to reality.

## Haves and have-nots redux

As Ross Baird has shown in his *The Innovation Blind Spot: Why we back the wrong ideas – and what to do about it*,[5] the stark reality is that startups always need funding to have a shot at becoming a disruptor. Yes, there are stories of startup entrepreneurs that have built massive successes with almost nothing to start with and only from cash flow, but there are few (very few) cases where this is literally true. Uncomfortably, many startups have been partly or wholly bankrolled by people like rich parents, investment banker-wives or -husbands, or similar funders. For the people unfortunate enough not to have been born into money and who've failed to marry into it, there are of course things like business angels and venture capital, but what Baird shows is that this money disproportionately goes to a specific sub-set of people with the 'right' background – particularly young Caucasian and Asian men who've gone to the 'right' universities. Yes, there are cases where uneducated African-American women have received venture capital, but they represent outliers. Thus even becoming a startup with the possibility for disruption is often a case of either benefitting from or battling against privilege.

Even if we ignore this point and the number of startups that never get off the ground because of what their founders lacked – the right family, the right background, the right connections, or the right look – there are still issues of privilege to consider. For all the ill that is spoken of them, large organizations have a number of resources that put them at a considerable advantage. Even if they were cash strapped, large corporations tend to have access to funding opportunities that startups can only dream of. When not cash strapped, they can easily fund experiments in innovation that small enterprises can only dream of. Large corporations have access to a talent pool that makes most small companies seem like shallow puddles (without in the least denigrating the talented people in e.g. startups). Few small companies can afford to hire technical specialists in highly niche fields, and, in addition, corporations can and do set up collaborations with top scientists in universities, gaining access to cutting-edge research (often at highly advantageous prices). Large organizations have broad and strong institutional networks, including but not limited to logistics chains, incumbent sales networks that can block or limit new entrants, existing contracts with suppliers and existing investments in things like production facilities. Granted, the latter can be both a boon and a hindrance, but overall innovation is easier when you have a lot of stuff in place and resources to play with than when you have neither. And note that we've not even addressed two key enablers of value extraction in modern economies – lobbying and lawyers.

Innovation might look like the way anyone can get ahead, no matter how big or small. Often it is yet another case of everyone being equal, just some being more equal than others. This is of course a discussion that is rarely broached in the traditional innovation literature and is kept rather quiet by the innovation industry. The latter knows full well who its customer is and really, *really* doesn't want to rock the boat. It has made a ton of money from peddling rags-to-riches stories about plucky startups and heroic young men, so it has little interest in presenting alternative takes. Even when it might be harming innovation in the process.

> *Often it is yet another case of everyone being equal, just some being more equal than others.*

## The innovations of privilege

I am very aware that this discussion may have rubbed you up the wrong way. You might now harbour a suspicion that I'm out to get men and in particular white men. You might think that I'm mean and unfair for presenting Steve Jobs in a light that isn't quite the normal halo reserved for secular saints. I understand, but note that nothing I write above is written to diminish anyone (except maybe the innovation industry). On the contrary, I wish for more people like Steve Jobs. It's just that I'd like to have more Gertrude Elions as well. Not to mention those tens of thousands of potential innovators that never got to step up to the plate because they didn't quite look the part.

My contention, in this chapter and in this book as a whole, is that innovation has suffered from being too narrowly defined, too shallow in its approach. This can be seen very clearly through the lens of diversity. What Ross Baird argues is that by primarily funding startups founded by white (or Asian) young men from specific universities, we miss out on all the innovation that could have been created by founders from other backgrounds. What neither he nor I argue is that you shouldn't get funding because you're a white young man – unless your idea is worse than that of for instance an older woman from the Indian subcontinent, in which case you certainly shouldn't. In a similar vein, it would of course be silly to claim that it is a problem that large organizations have access to resources and can use these for innovation initiatives. What needs to be raised, however, is that in both cases, innovation can become skewed.

A climate of startup funding that gives an advantage to young men has created a plethora of innovations (or 'innovations') that solve problems that young and relatively affluent men might have: there is no lack of apps for home delivery of food nor of dating apps. There has never been a greater time to be a gamer than today, with a dizzying amount of wonderful games and delightful peripherals to buy. If your key problem is how to keep in touch with your bros, you don't need to fret. If your problems extend beyond how to keep entertained, getting pizza delivered and paying for porn anonymously with cryptocurrencies, you're not quite as well cared for. Silicon Valley – which today is less a geographical area than it is a mindset – isn't quite as interested in poor single women as it is in the issues befalling middle-aged men of means (and again, I know I'm talking against my own self-interest). Non-Caucasian consumers might not be actively discouraged by the innovation industry, as it can be quite democratic when it comes to good ol'-fashioned greed, but they aren't necessarily courted, as Baird highlights. And if you're something as unfortunate as old or dealing with being differently abled, do not be surprised if the mantras regarding solving wicked problems don't seem to apply to you. Come on, there are smart home technologies for optimizing the man-cave experience to invent!

When it comes to large corporations and B2B, the picture might not look quite as bleak. Diagnostics technology mostly transcends human variability, and industrial valves are themselves rarely ageist. That said, the innovation cultures of companies creating such solutions can still miss out on utilizing the full spectrum of their cognitive surplus, simply by focusing more on the ideas of those seen as 'innovative' – primarily young white males – rather than engaging all of their employees. On a very real level, innovation is a numbers game, and the company with the most ideas wins. The company that only takes the ideas of a specific minority into account is effectively handicapping itself, and the scary thing is that it might not even realize that this is what it is doing.

## Moving beyond male, pale and stale

The lack of diversity in much of the innovation discussion is not merely a moral or political problem. It is, in a very real way, a triple threat to companies, something that can hit their bottom line in three separate if interwoven ways. One, a lack of diversity in innovation all but guarantees only directing innovation efforts to a relatively limited segment of the market. Two, low levels of diversity in an organization lead directly to a diminished set of new and novel ideas, by dint of the self-evident fact that having more people with varying backgrounds and perspectives will always lead to a wider array of ideas. Three, and for some most convincingly, the data shows that diversity and inclusion have a measurable impact on bottom lines.

In 2018, McKinsey released a report on *Delivering Through Diversity*[6] that showed just how much diversity can contribute to financial performance. It showed that companies that are more gender-diverse than their competitors do a whopping 21 per cent better than their peers, performance-wise. Not only that, companies that show a strong degree of diversity when it comes to ethnicity outperform their peers by 33 per cent. In a business environment where even tenths of a percentage point matter, these are cataclysmic figures. Cataclysmic, but not difficult to understand. I mean, this is what self-evidently happens if you ignore segments of the market and limit the number of new ideas that emerge from the organization.

This is why we can speak about 'a diversity dividend', a measurable uptick in both financial and other results in organizations that have a high degree of diversity. This is not to say that non-diverse organizations cannot have good results, because they can. However, it is highly likely that they too would have generated even better results with added diversity. Do, however, note that diversity is a more complex

> *We can speak about 'a diversity dividend', a measurable uptick in both financial and other results in organizations that have a high degree of diversity.*

and, yes, diverse concept than many people give it credit for. Yes, gender diversity and diversity when it comes to ethnicities are major categories. They are not, however, the only such.

In fact, I've warned against the tendency to think solely of these categories. In many of the organizations I've worked with, particularly the bigger corporations, there has been at least a

modicum of attention placed on the aforementioned two categories. However, this was often tempered by a tendency to emphasize
educational background or 'time served' in the organization.
When working for a major insurance company, for instance, I
noted that whilst they worked hard to hire in a more diverse way,
they by some unspoken contract focused their search specifically
on people with a 'safe' educational background, i.e. looking for
diverse hires almost solely from top universities. Similarly, when
attempting to address diversity in their promotions, they still
retained a curious bias by primarily applying this to individuals
from under-represented categories who had been with the organization for longer periods of time. In other words, once they had
been around for long enough to adapt to the corporate culture
and effectively de-diversified themselves...

In other words, most corporations still have a lot of work ahead
of them when it comes to diversity. To truly create a culture of deep
creativity, we need many kinds of diversity, including cognitive
diversity. This is not to devalue or diminish the importance of
gender diversity, but rather in fact to enhance it. It isn't enough
that women are hired and women are being promoted; for an
innovation culture we need to ensure that a multitude of women
are respected and heard: introverted and extroverted, from privileged backgrounds and less so, nerds as well as cool types, with
various educations, experience and ages. And, of course, women
from various ethnic backgrounds and people with various ways of
identifying, including those who may have a complex way of identifying with gender and those who exist outside of cisnormative
ideas about the gender binary. The cognitive surplus available
when truly embracing diversity contains multitudes.

## The one thing we know about innovative teams

The term *monoculture* was originally used in agriculture to refer
to the practice of cultivating only a single crop on a single field

or even farm. It has gone on to be applied to any system that has a low degree of diversity, and I use it here to describe organizations where a specific group is either quantitatively or functionally dominant. For a good example of monocultures, we could look to any number of the Silicon Valley companies routinely celebrated by the innovation industry. Whilst many have at least tried to work on their diversity, the fact is that many of these (including some of the very best known) are still dominated by young men, often with a degree in engineering and primarily Caucasian or Asian. Interestingly, many of these are now showing signs of not being able to keep up with their previous reputation for innovation, and some are floundering.

It should of course come as no surprise that innovation fatigue can be enhanced by a sense of not being appreciated and respected, simply because you are not part of a group that has been labelled 'innovative'. For example, if only engineers are seen as capable of innovation, basically every other group in the organization will feel at least some sense of innovation fatigue. This is why psychological safety, i.e. the feeling that even those outside the monoculture can have a voice, is so very powerful as a predictor of innovation. Interestingly, the research of Alison Reynolds and David Lewis[7] has indicated that this is only one side of the story.

Teams with a high degree of psychological safety are good spaces to nurture ideas, and they often show a high degree of appreciation for ideas and consideration for others. However, they do not necessarily rate highly when it comes to curiosity and experimentation. To achieve this, Reynolds and Lewis argue that teams must also have a high degree of cognitive diversity. This term obviously covers a lot of ground, and they define it as 'differences in perspective or information processing styles',[8] i.e. having a high degree of cognitive diversity means that you have people with very different ways of approaching problems. They further note that this is a form of diversity that isn't directly correlated with other forms of diversity – it is fully possible to have a team that is very diverse in every other manner *except* their cognitive approach (which could therefore still hamper them).

Reynolds and Lewis thus argue that we need both psychological safety (to ensure that ideas aren't routinely killed) and cognitive diversity (to ensure that ideas are developed in the best possible ways). Whilst they do not address this directly, once these are in place, other forms of diversity are of course productive as well, for a number of reasons including but not limited to, having more perspectives on a problem and being able to spot problems or challenges that might otherwise remain invisible.

## On the fine art of respectful disharmony

All this might read like a particularly starry-eyed take on teams and innovation, one where the aim is to create something akin to a Woodstock with peace, love and harmony (amongst the flower children). This is very far from the truth. It is true that cultures of deep creativity demand that people behave respectfully towards each other. It is also true that psychological safety is important if a company wishes to engage people in innovation. But this does not mean that everything needs or even should be smiles and lollipops. Quite the contrary.

As research into team work has shown time and time again,[9] a degree of disharmony, conflict and constraints actually makes teams *more* creative. With nothing but respect and psychological safety, a team becomes anodyne and uncreative. With nothing to temper disharmony and conflict, a team becomes toxic and pathological. What is needed then, for a team to escape shallow creativity, is the art of ***respectful disharmony***. What this refers to is a set of behaviours in which a team can communicate about difficult things and disagreements, but to do so in a manner that retains a respectful manner and a reciprocity. In other words, not merely criticism for the sake of criticism.

Here, diversity can somewhat surprisingly be a strong agent of reaching such a state. The problem with cognitive diversity can be that people simply fail to understand that there is true diversity present. This can in turn lead to a diminished respect between the team members, pushing disharmony to problematic levels. With a greater 'visible' diversity, this can be abated as team members need to negotiate their differences and are more likely to test their assumptions about the other parties.

This, however, is easier on the level of teams and more difficult on the organizational level. Here, leaders must learn to think in a broader manner about how cultures can negotiate respectful disharmony on an organizational level and how different modes of diversity can co-exist and intermingle.

## Rise of the culture brokers

Throughout this book, I have argued that organizations have a tremendous amount of under-utilized cognitive surplus, which is currently repressed by shallow attempts at innovation, a general innovation fatigue, as well as sub-optimal cultures and organizational forms. What we haven't addressed is that this cognitive surplus can become isolated into islands and bubbles that rarely engage in the important act of creative cross-pollination. On an organizational level, and for the creation of a culture of deep creativity, this means that a number of processes of negotiation, translation and brokerage need to be deployed to materialize the diversity dividend.

In her research on creative performance in diverse teams, Sujin Jang focuses on this specific fact and argues for the need for 'cultural brokers' to fully utilize the potential in diversity and to ably navigate the potential issues in multicultural collaboration.[10] Such cultural brokers ease interactions by dint of having more multicultural experience, and Jang shows that when teams have members that can act as such a broker, they are also measurably more creative. This is because the act of cultural brokerage can lead to both merging ideas from more than one culture and enhancing the sharing of ideas and cultural experience more broadly – both of which improve creative output.

Looking back to the elements of a deep innovation culture, this makes a lot of sense. Cultural brokerage enhances reciprocity, the ongoing give and take in teams, and also enhances internal respect in a team. The fact that a cultural broker, by their very nature, should increase psychological safety obviously helps as well. Jang's research focuses specifically on ethnicity and national cultures, but could easily be extended beyond this. On an organizational level, there may well be a need for many kinds of cultural brokerage, even in organizations with few national cultures represented.

This is because there are many potential splits and divisions within a company that may need their own forms of translation. Age, educational or socio-economic background, even positions on the introvert/extrovert scale can all put up barriers for a deep sharing of ideas, and overcoming such often requires a concentrated effort. At one point I worked with a software company that produced integrated backend solutions for industrial use. The team tasked with the development of these solutions were all software engineers and embraced this as an identity marker to an almost comical degree. Management, somewhat confusingly, consisted mainly of people with either a sales background or with a long experience in industry, but not necessarily in coding and software. This separation, more than any other, affected communication and innovation in the company, and, according to the CEO, the situation got worse over the period of a year.

In my interviews, it was at first unclear what had caused this, and neither the coding team nor the management team offered up any suggestions. That is, until someone let slip that it had become more difficult when a person named Michael had left the company. I talked to the coders who agreed that Michael had left, but didn't see this as particularly important as he was a relatively junior coder. Neither did management immediately see that he would have been all that central. One of them did laughingly say that Michael had been a nice guy and continued, 'he was sort of a nerd-whisperer'. When I asked what he meant by this, he seemed to remember something and started talking about how Michael had often explained technical issues in meetings 'in a way that humans understand' and how he seemed to be able to communicate the wishes of management to his fellow 'nerds'. When I checked with the programmers, they too agreed that Michael had been good at understanding 'the nonsense management came with'. In other words, the organization had lost a key cultural broker without realizing it or even fully knowing that they had one to begin with.

## A band of brokers

An organization may therefore need an entire band of people who engage in cultural brokerage. Obviously, management should at all times be attentive to ideas from various parts of the organization (and outside it), but this isn't always enough. What leaders need to do is identify those who are like the aforementioned Michael, people who despite not necessarily having a formal position as such still translate between groups and across barriers.

Particularly when working with larger corporations, I often encourage CEOs to list who might hold such informal roles, and in particular who can connect groups that are very far apart. Consider your own organization. Do you have a 'nerd-whisperer' (as an aside I might mention that I am a dyed-in-the-wool nerd, have been one since childhood and feel I can use the term without prejudice – for my people), that is someone who can connect people with deep knowledge in a specialization such as IT or material science with people in areas such as sales or HR? Do you have someone who 'speaks millennial' and who can act as a connector between your younger staff and top management and even the board?

This is not to say that such positions are easy; neither that they can be filled by fiat. Rather, which Jang has also suggested, leaders need to ensure that the company culture is such that there is support for cultural brokers. This of course also includes respecting and rewarding the people who take on such roles. Too often, people who act as translators between different groups in organizations find themselves simply tasked with more and more work, without seeing any real compensation for the often hard work that they do.

At play here, as so many times before, is that the innovation industry has skewed our vision of what innovation and a strong innovation culture require. We don't need one more model. Most of the time, we don't need one more initiative or competition. We need people and connections between them. We don't need a process to 'weed out bad ideas'; we need a culture in which ideas are cared for and nurtured. In fact, we often don't need management as much as we need compassion.

## An aside on compassion

Recently, in social theory more broadly and increasingly in organization and management studies as well, there has been a great deal of interest in the concept of *affect*. Today we can even talk of affect theory. Here, I am referring to the philosophical use of the word, which might best be described as dealing with shared emotional states that we often experience not so much analytically but in an embodied sense. If this sounds like jargon, an example might be helpful. Have you ever walked into a meeting or similar and felt that the atmosphere was very tense, but you didn't really know why? Or joined a party and it just felt like the kind of place where you're guaranteed to have a good time? Or walked into a bar and felt it to be vaguely menacing and dangerous? If you haven't, you really need to get out more, but if you have you've experienced affect without having a word for it. Those feelings, which we pick up not so much by objectively analysing a situation but more through our bodies' wonderful capacity to pick up on minute things, connect to an affect.

It can be in the way people's bodies are tense and their smiles fake, or in the way people hold their heads and hands. It can be just the smallest twitch, but even though we process it more without bodies and our gut, we can pick up on it. I've already addressed one version of all this in Chapter 2, where the notion of micro-behaviours and their capacity to dampen and kill an innovation culture was discussed. Compassion, as an affect, could be seen as the positive version of this. A shared feeling of care between people, an openness that isn't so much stated as it is experienced.

What cultural brokerage does is opens up people's eyes to other ways of understanding the world and to the manner in which we all carry biases and preconceived notions. Through this, first a team and then an organization can start looking at the world in a way that is a little more open to the ideas of others, a little more respectful of diverging opinions, a little more prepared to engage in a reciprocal process of give and take. This is not something that can be programmed or easily measured but something that needs to be *sensed* in an organization. You will know you've succeeded when people actually communicate, through their eyes and gestures just as much as through their words, that they care not only about people's ideas but also about the people themselves.

## From diversity to impact

Diversity, then, isn't so much something you can add on when the company can afford it. It is a critical part of any innovation culture. Without differences in approach and perspective, coupled with the right amount of respectful disharmony and the broker-ing of connections between different standpoints, deep innovation will not emerge. You might create some shallow innovation, like the often me-too inno-vations that today emerge out of the 'brotopia' that is Silicon Valley, but innovations with impact require some-thing more. They demand having an organization that not only has a deep technical expertise but a deep lived one and the compassion to respect and utilize it.

*Diversity isn't so much something you can add on when the company can afford it. It is a critical part of any innovation culture.*

This is also how the link between diversity and meaning in innovative organizations emerges. The focus and shared perspec-tive of monocultures can quickly turn into superficiality and myopia, a fate that has beset many companies trying to take the leap from punchy startup to a growing, stable company. As a company is forced to engage with more than their own core team and their original customer group, what was once a strength can rapidly turn into a critical weakness. Just consider Uber or WeWork, both companies that have shown explosive growth, but which have also been criticized for a 'frat-boy culture'. Whilst both still carry high valuations, both have also had to field ques-tions regarding whether their business model of selling ease of living to the already privileged is sustainable in the long run.[11]

In such a context, which is also the context within which a great many innovation books are written, talking about innova-tion and the plight of low-income, single mothers seems like a paradox. The latter might have problems but not of the kind that shallow innovation cultures are interested in solving. The same goes for a number of disadvantaged groups, including but not limited to war veterans, the elderly, numerous groups dealing with discrimination, migrants and, increasingly, people from a rural background. As these groups often have limited representation in innovation teams (not to mention books on innovation), privilege keeps reaffirming itself. Note that I am not saying this to attack people who design yet another service to ease the already considerably eased life of well-to-do urbanites such as myself. Companies will often go where the easy money is. I do, however, say that this shows that what we call 'innovation' isn't some kind of general good, but often a good to a very well-defined group. A group whose sons and daughters then go to the right schools and end up on the innovation teams that create the next generation of urbanite comfort services.

Thus we return to how innovation can break out of the 'blind spot' Ross Baird named his book after. For although the often marginalized groups mentioned here have been overlooked by the innovation industry, that doesn't mean that they do not represent a tremendous innovation opportunity. Looking just to the notion of the elderly, the AARP (formerly American Association of Retired Persons) together with Oxford Economics have in a report entitled *The Longevity Economy*[12] estimated that US spending by those over 50 will increase by 58 per cent over the period to 2040, compared with 24 per cent by those in the group 25 to 50. It takes neither a genius nor a professor (or, although they are rare, a genius professor) to figure out the opportunity this represents. And this isn't even the worst blind spot.

## Making innovation meaningful

Recall that we looked to just how much we globally spend on innovation. The *lowest* estimate is a hair-raising US $3,000,000,000,000. That's enough money to give US $400 to every person on the planet. If only distributed to people falling under the definition of 'extreme poverty', they would get almost US $4,000. Then again, we wouldn't have electric scooters. So there's that.

We are of course not able to direct money in such an easy way. I merely state this to once again remind you just how much we spend on innovation globally (and note, I used the lowball figure). We have all that money to spend and more highly educated people than ever before in history. Basically, everyone who has picked up this book owns not one but two supercomputers (yes, your smartphone counts). At a minimum. Almost everyone who lives in a developed country has access to more information than they can possibly use, usually accessible from both of the aforementioned supercomputers. And yet, for all this, 800,000 children will die this year from... diarrhoea.[13] Yes, in the same world that the technology optimists hail as a golden age of innovation, and with all our riches, we've yet to figure out how to make sure children have access to water that doesn't kill them.

This is why issues of diversity and compassion aren't just pretty ideas but critical parts of bringing meaning back to innovation. To bring in a diversity of perspectives that can challenge the glib tales of the innovation industry. To push back against ways of talking about innovation that manage to simultaneously sing its praises without taking it seriously. This is why we will now turn to courage and meaning and ambition. Innovation beyond the nonsense, if you will.

CHAPTER SIX

# Making innovation resilient

*Meaning, purpose, ambition, courage*

'We do not measure a culture by its output of undisguised trivialities but by what it claims as significant.' NEIL POSTMAN

## When innovation becomes bullshit

In 1986, the philosopher Harry Frankfurt wrote an essay entitled *On Bullshit.*[1] In this he argued that the term, which might sound offensive to some, raised interesting philosophical questions, not least as the phenomenon is so widespread. The essay, which was later published as a book and became a minor bestseller, argued that bullshit, rather than being an inappropriate word, in fact perfectly described a particular kind of relationship with truth. Frankfurt points out that bullshit is interesting specifically because it is not a lie. A lie is a false statement where the person stating it knows it is false and which further can be checked against the evidence. For instance, I could say that I am a young Japanese girl, who in addition is a championship gymnast. I know I'm not, and frankly, anyone who sees me will consider it a particularly clumsy lie. That notwithstanding, Frankfurt says, it is still in one sense a relationship with the truth, if a skewed one.

Bullshit, on the other hand, is something else entirely. It is rather 'unconnected to a concern with the truth', in Frankfurt's turn of phrase. It is a statement offered in order to persuade the listener but not necessarily about the matter at hand. A key characteristic of bullshit is that it is offered in order for the person who speaks it to elevate him- or herself in the eyes of others. The politician's waffle, the professor's highfalutin turns of phrase and the priest's empty homilies can all be examples of this. Here, language is not used to carry truth or even falsehood, just hot air with an aim to impress or bamboozle the audience.

Now, we all know that there is a lot of business bullshit. There are entire books devoted to this, such as my friend André Spicer's *Business Bullshit,*[2] and we can all recall egregious cases we've come across personally. What is interesting in our specific context is just how much innovation bullshit there is. There are the empty phrases, the fancy terminologies, the constant misquotes. Entire projects full of it, in fact.


## Draped in innovation talk

In 2013 I did a project together with a major retailer, one where the top management team was utterly taken by the theories of disruptive innovation as originally developed by Clayton Christensen and later misrepresented by a bevy of management consultants. Their preferred consultant in this field was a very well-dressed man from the UK, one with a bestselling innovation book to his name. He was brought in both for all-company conferences, where he gave keynote speeches with great gusto, and to run workshops with the management team, where he continuously urged the team to 'be more disruptive'. This, in itself, was not a problem. What was a problem, however, is that his definition of what 'being disruptive' was changed quite radically from time to time. In his keynote speeches he had a tendency to urge his listeners to 'challenge everything' and list any number of currently popular companies and/or products as being 'disruptive innovators'. This included companies that introduced completely new products, companies that added on services in order to raise their prices, companies that were sold off before they'd delivered a product to market, and several other variations on the theme. Being a mere humble professor of innovation, I could not make out what united these except the consultant's bright-eyed insistence that they were all innovators and disruptors. This was also proven by a series of slides where innovation was placed at the centre and all other functions twirled around it – clockwise. Always clockwise. With arrows. Lots and lots of arrows. Interestingly, if not a little infuriatingly, innovation was also supposed to be both the core competence of the company and, simultaneously, the force that 'blasts away' the foundations of the company. How you can establish a sound structure by having explosives at the core was not fully explained.

In the workshops, similar pablum was brought out, if in a slightly less pompous manner. Here, the consultant focused more on the mantra of 'do it differently'. This, he stated, was the core of disruptive innovation. Now, this would probably have come as something of a surprise to Clayton Christensen, whose theories were being so liberally (mis-)quoted, as his notion built primarily on doing something surprisingly similar, if with a twist that made this available for a new market, or as he has put it himself:

> Generally, disruptive innovations were technologically
> straightforward, consisting of off-the-shelf components put
> together in a product architecture that was often simpler than prior

approaches. They offered less of what customers in established markets wanted and so could rarely be initially employed there. They offered a different package of attributes valued only in emerging markets remote from, and unimportant to, the mainstream.[3]

Arguably, doing it 'differently' would cover such instances as well, but the consultant in this tale was not to be limited by anything as trivial as the theory. Instead, he urged the management team to consider 'all possibilities, particularly the crazy ones' and urged them to be seen as 'the wild men of retail'. Whenever one of the less easily enthused members of the team questioned this, they were told that the theory of disruptive innovation proves that it is only those companies that throw themselves wholeheartedly into 'destroying their current business before someone else does' who will survive. This, and similar mind-boggling misrepresentations of theories of innovation – which, in case you're interested, are often much more pedestrian than their interlocutors would have you believe – went on for some time. In the end, the innovation expert, for all his marketing material insisted that he was, finished the workshop by pointing out that the company needed to develop a culture in which 'revolutions happen daily', where 'mistakes are celebrated', which 'fails faster' and which 'always disrupts'.

Our expert here is a prime example of a bullshitter. He had, it has to be pointed out, read some innovation theory. He had, or at least I think so, at some point understood what he read. Many of the things he said had at least a kernel of truth to them, even if this kernel was often popped out of all proportion. He was exceptionally good at repeating the kind of phrases that we expect to hear from an innovation talk, and he referenced a number of famous thinkers and CEOs to bolster his argument. Put somewhat differently, he had all the right moves, said all the right things, referenced all the right people and still none of it hung together to make a coherent whole. He was, in a sense, draped in innovation talk, and that, to him, seemed to be enough. Sense or coherence were less important to him than positioning yourself as a legitimate pundit in the field by making the right symbolic gestures – which is why he had no problem presenting keynote speeches making wildly divergent and contradictory points and shooing away questions regarding all this by stating: 'Innovation is all about embracing paradoxes'.

## Bringing meaning back in

What the kind of innovation bullshit described above does is that it slowly but surely empties the concept of meaning. When absolutely everything can be called an innovation, the term becomes less and less meaningful. It becomes an empty marker, used more to convey status and being with the in-crowd than anything else. It becomes just a label that can be stuck onto almost anything, no matter how meaningless. Consider for instance the 'smarter socks' from Blacksocks™, somewhat redundantly branded as Plus+. These are regular black socks, but equipped with sensors that can communicate with an app on your iPhone. This innovation comes with many benefits, including aiding in sorting and pairing, being able to check how often the socks have been washed, not to mention that the app 'can also tell you if your black socks are no longer properly black and help you buy new socks'.[4] This kind of over-solving non-problems comes naturally in a world where innovation, as a concept, has become so profoundly detached from notions of meaning and sense.

*When absolutely everything can be called an innovation, the term becomes meaningless.*

What I now claim is that all this is connected with how innovation fatigue can be seen as a symptom of a more troubling ailment.

If we look to the business world more generally, a key finding in several studies has been that people no longer find that their jobs, or their organizations, are particularly meaningful. David Graeber, the radical US anthropologist, deftly captured this *Zeitgeist* in his *Bullshit Jobs: A Theory,*[5] where he argued that a great deal of the jobs that exist today are quite meaningless and exist mainly to keep people busy and to keep the corporations looking powerful. Whilst his position is somewhat extreme – he seems to suggest that all of financial services, not to mention PR, has no point whatsoever – he also manages to put his finger on a sensation a lot of people share. There are bullshit jobs (including in the innovation industry), and there is an emptying out of meaning in modern work, including in the innovation sphere. In a study conducted by Gallup, it was stated that only 15 per cent of employees globally are engaged with their work, whereas the rest are either unengaged or actively disengaged. Two in three employees were categorized as being indifferent to their work – with all the problems this brings with it.

Experiencing a lack of meaning in your job can lead to a range of afflictions. It has been shown to lead to a loss of productivity, increased absenteeism and increased turnover in staff. If any of this surprises you, you might be part of the problem. Still, as glaringly self-evident as these dispatches from Captain Obvious are, they are still not addressed with enough seriousness in the innovation literature. Experiencing a lack of meaning about innovation as well compounds this and can make people become despondent and cynical. With enough people feeling this way, this starts defining the organizational culture itself.

## Meaning, purpose, leadership

What this means for leaders is that whilst it is important to make sure that the basic cultural values for nurturing and developing ideas are in place, and that the organization has the requisite diversity and willingness to think imaginatively, you need to make innovation meaningful as well. And whilst many CEOs seem to think that this is self-evident, the data paints a different picture. As stated in the earlier paragraph, only about a third of employees feel engaged with their jobs, and nothing indicates that the result would be any better when talking about innovation. In fact, quite a lot indicates the opposite.

To succeed, companies need to think less about innovation in general and more about what the *purpose* of their innovation activities is. Whilst the term purpose is bandied about in the broader management literature, it plays a decidedly less prominent role in popular innovation books. This is in line with the notions of innovation as inherently doable and as a reason unto itself that is prevalent in the innovation industry. What it has led to, however, is a tendency amongst executives to simply call for their organizations to be more innovative without clarifying, beyond the profit motive, *why* they should. This, coupled with several other trends in the business world, has then resulted in great amounts of decidedly non-innovative 'innovation'.

> *To succeed, companies need to think less about innovation in general and more about what the purpose of their innovation activities is.*

One example of this can be seen in how a limited set of developments has become something of a blueprint for how many companies approach innovation. Popular terms such as *digitalization*, *business model* and *freemium* have in the popular discourse all been intimately connected with innovation, and as a result we've seen no end of corporations launching one or more apps, attempting various plays on the freemium strategy and endlessly poring over their business model canvases. As a further result, there are at the moment of writing over 800,000 games in the iTunes Store, only several dozen of which seem truly original. There are also 2.5 million apps, most of which seem to run primarily on 'in-app purchases' (coming soon to a pacemaker near you![6]). There is a never-ending barrage of same, same, same.

We get sameness when we lack a purpose with what we're doing and when we simply attend to the superficial qualities of innovation. We hear that blockchain is innovative, so we try to use blockchain. We hear it's innovative to have an app, so we try to launch one. But in doing so, we are actually just mimicking innovation. Worse yet, we're mimicking what is innovation to someone else. To break with this, we need to be able to call out nonsense as nonsense and find the things that make engaging with innovation meaningful for the organizational culture.

## Innovation cultures thrive on meaning

The observation that purpose can help drive innovation is of course not wholly original. EY, working with Harvard Business School and the Economist Intelligence Unit, has long championed the need for purpose to drive businesses. They note in a survey of executives that 63.4 per cent stated that a sense of purpose supported their innovation capabilities and helped them deal with disruption.[7] Another study, conducted by the Harvard Business Review Analytic Services, stated that 73 per cent of surveyed executives said purpose drove innovation and positive change.[8] That said, this oft-stated understanding of the importance of purpose for a business doesn't always translate into meaningful action.

One of my personal favourites in this genre is the US company I once did a keynote speech for, after which I had the chance to dine with the CEO. He was gregarious and said some nice things about my talk and particularly latched onto the fact that I had emphasized the role of a strong purpose for a company wanting to innovate. He said that he whole-heartedly agreed and that this was why he had made sure that everyone in his company knew the purpose of it. I asked him to share this with me and with no little amount of pride he said, 'Excellence!' I was a little bewildered, so I asked what he meant, and he went on to explain that the purpose of his company was excellence in all that they did. I seriously didn't know what to say. Whilst I guess that this can be called a purpose on a technical level, it obviously doesn't go very far in creating meaning for the organization. Think about it. You are told to innovate (which can mean just about anything) and then told to do it in a manner that lives up to the purpose of 'excellence'. The likelihood you'll just give up, as all you're getting in the form of guidance are vacuous buzzwords, has just skyrocketed.

Compare this to Bempu. This is a company in the field of neonatal care, with a particular focus on India. Their flagship product is a low-cost bracelet that monitors the body temperature of babies during their first months. It is, in effect, a warning system for hypothermia in babies, which is a major killer in the developing world, and which can also affect later development in a child. The founder, Ratul Narain, stated:

> I wanted to create something that would have a massive impact. With the neonatal space, we are trying to make the biggest impact we can in people's lives and their health. If you make a difference to a baby's life, it actually has a drastic impact on the next 60–80 years of their life.[9]

This same sense of purpose can be gleaned in the tagline the company uses – 'Simply saving lives'. Such a purpose, enriched with lived values, enables the company to both grow the impact of their original innovation and communicate a meaningful innovation message. What engages more, being part of saving lives or an exhortation to be generally, abstractly excellent?

## Just enough stress

In the introduction to this book, we discussed the forms innovation cultures can take, and in doing so highlighted *shallow* and *show-off* cultures. These are cultures that both care more about novelties than impact and are more engaged with whether their innovation will generate good PR than actually engendering change. What holds such cultures back is that they are more preoccupied with the novelty aspect of an innovation than the impact it might have. Succinctly put, they represent innovation cultures that have a very low level of *innovation ambition*.

Now, ambition is a dynamic that is easy to misunderstand, and an exhortation for ambition is easy to overdo. As in so many other things, having none is a bad thing, but having unreasonably much isn't great either. As research in creativity has shown, optimal results usually come from constraints[10] rather than total freedom. Where having too little time will hinder creativity, so will having too much.[11] Similar effects have been identified in strategy. Strategy researchers Carsten Lund Pedersen and Thomas Ritter have argued that the execution of strategies contains an element of tension and 'strategic stress'.[12] When this is too low, i.e. when the strategy is easily executed and targets aren't a challenge to reach, the company will suffer 'strategic boredom'. On the other hand, when strategies are unrealistic and market forces rather than a plan guide the company, it will experience 'strategic burnout'. The best-case scenario, they argue, is one where there is enough stress and tension in the execution of the strategy that the company and the individuals in it feel challenged 'by a sufficient balance between alignment and nonconformity'.[13]

This dynamic plays out in innovation as well, and the situation is often exacerbated by the fact that innovation as a concept has become so vague that it is difficult to tell from individual instances of management communication what kinds of innovations are required and requested! In other words, when a CEO states that they expect everyone to think in innovative ways, a series of things can happen in the organization. Some will react with boredom, others with burnout. If the message isn't specified in more detail, it will primarily cause confusion. The trick here is to find a balance and with clear examples communicate what level, kind and variety of innovation is desired. In other words, leaders must learn how to communicate *an innovation ambition that is aligned with a company's purpose, enough to energize, but not so unrealistic as to depress.*

## Innovation ambition

The point of thinking in terms of innovation ambition can be understood on two levels. On a general, societal level, we can discuss what the level of innovation ambition of currently celebrated companies is and whether this is sufficient. Here we might state that the innovation ambition in a pair of Plus+ black socks, or yet another freemium app with which you can share photos, is rather low. Their technological solution might be fantastic, their user experience to die for, but this alone doth not an impactful innovation make. We can then further discuss what level of innovation ambition we might expect from companies and organizations and even return to the issue of what a proper ROII (Return on Innovation Investment, which doesn't need to be purely financial) might look like in society.

On an organizational level, innovation ambition is a way to ensure that innovation connects to a company's purpose, rather than being a set of superficial exercises primarily designed to prove that the company is in line with prevailing innovation ideologies. It can also be understood as a measure of whether what the company is doing deserves the right to be called 'innovation', or whether this has become just more grist for the marketing mill. If we for instance look back to the case of Kellogg's, which wanted to present a peanut butter-flavoured Pop-Tart as an innovation, the best internal response this should have received should have been an incredulous guffaw. What it might have done after this, to the benefit of the innovation culture in Kellogg's, would have been to spark a serious discussion in the company about what goals innovation is supposed to achieve, beyond slightly improved sales and some media mentions.

What the term should stand for, then, is not so much a prescriptive level of innovation that an organization is supposed to reach. Such a notion of innovation might sit well with pundits in the innovation industry, but it is fatally flawed. As innovation will always transcend simple metrics, our task in organizations is quite different from setting a distinct target of number of patents or additional revenue. Rather, it should be to openly discuss what isn't good enough, even if it drives revenue or amasses patents, and what kind of innovation talk is simply fantasy. From such a discussion we can start finding the kinds of ambitions that would be meaningful, both by representing a deep engagement with the purpose of the organization and by not creating a sensation of impossibility and fatigue.

One of my favourite cases is from Anti-Germ, a leading company in food safety. Founded in Memmingen in Germany, it is today a top international company in the business of food safety, providing such things as detergents, disinfectants and services for dairies, farms and the food and beverage industry. Their CEO, Matthias Kötter, openly acknowledges the challenge of being in a business where biocides (highly regulated poisonous substances needed to combat germs and fungi in food) figure prominently and therefore likes to highlight their work with Aquatabs, a product of their subsidiary Medentech. These are a cheap and easy solution for creating drinkable water in countries where much of the drinking water is dirty. Consisting of tablets that can be put into highly contaminated water to make it potable, this is likely today the leading water-purification tablet in the world. Used by international NGOs in some of the poorest countries in the world, they have by now saved countless lives and quite literally lessened the number of children who die from diarrhoea.

What is important to note here is the effect a product like this can have on the overall culture. Rather than keeping wedded to their traditional customers in the food industry, the company wanted to emphasize that they did something more ambitious than ensuring that beverages lived up to standards set by the authorities. In other words, they wanted to make innovation meaningful in their company, in order to strengthen their creative culture. By having an innovation such as the Aquatabs, and a CEO like Matthias Kötter who champions the same (he has a tendency to give them to anyone he meets who might be going somewhere with less than safe water), Anti-Germ makes a powerful statement that innovation can be something greater than yet another me-too product, even if your company works in a segment that isn't quite as sexy as IT or media. Sure, it's only chemicals. But it's chemicals that save children.

## The safety of the shallows

Here, the reason why it is so much easier to just stick to shallow, me-too innovation needs to be addressed. Why did Anti-Germ pour resources into an innovation that doesn't really have the biggest margins rather than creating the world's first app for a blockchain-operated platform and social network for food safety chemicals? In short, because they had ambition and courage, because doing the latter had clearly been a lot safer. It would have received more PR, involved fewer negotiations with NGOs and had fewer logistics issues. In fact, most innovation consultants would have suggested they'd do the latter, because as twisted as it is, in the innovation industry digitalization is valorized, and children dying from unsafe water are rarely mentioned.

The truth of the matter is that shallow innovating is far safer than its deeper counterpart. As it will be easily recognized as 'innovation', it is more likely to receive positive write-ups in media and understanding nods from key stakeholders. Financial actors are more likely to reward investments in innovations if they can recognize them as such, and the same goes for the board of the company. The less known, i.e. the more imaginative the innovation project, the higher the likelihood of resistance and opposition.

Shallow innovation is also far easier. In a landmark paper called 'The iron cage revisited: institutional isomorphism and collective rationality in organizational fields',[14] Powell and DiMaggio highlight how organizations are in fact constantly looking to their competitors and the like for ideas about what to do next. This leads to a constant copying between organizations, or as expressed in academese, 'mimetic isomorphism'. One organization sets up a web-shop, and all the others attempt to do the same. One says they're looking into blockchain technology, and suddenly the demand for consultants with that as a specialization skyrockets. This follows simply from the fact that an innovation that has been legitimized by being adopted by a respected actor will be easier to adopt than a radically new one.

What a conversation about ambition and daring and courage can do is to start breaking with this – to engage the innovation culture to think beyond what kind of innovations win awards and press accolades, and instead start thinking in terms of impact and change, diverse customers and the jobs that still aren't done.

## Daring and caring

Ambition is, by definition, hard. To dare is, by definition, scary. Daring and caring both require courage. Not foolhardy courage, or the kind of courage where you run into a burning building to save a child, but courage nevertheless. The kind of courage where one dares to do the slightly more different thing, or the thing that doesn't elicit quite as many nods or has quite as many cheerleaders. For managers trying to create a culture of deep innovation, it also means building a foundation for the courage of others. This is because managers need to care for nurturing courage dovetails nicely with what we've so far said about respectful and responsible cultures.

*Ambition is, by definition, hard. To dare is, by definition, scary.*

The courage I address here then might best be understood as a kind of meta-courage, principles through which we can free the boldness that exists as a potential in an organization. When I come across an organization beset by innovation fatigue, I always remind myself that this doesn't mean that the people in it are against change, or are cowards or unimaginative. On the contrary, I know they are not. Instead, they are people with bold ideas who have lost faith in the organization being honest and truthful in their innovation discourse. They are people who still have courage, in theory, but who have been let down so often they no longer wish to use it – at least not at the place of their employ. These are the people that a wise manager who still wants the company to have innovation ambition focuses on.

To do this, I've found that there are three kinds of courage that managers and executives must engage with, in order to build bolder cultures. These do not cover everything – there are still incentives that need to be set and the need for continuous encouragement, to mention just two – but they are critical ones that are often forgotten or mishandled. The three are:

1  *The courage to allow;*
2  *The courage to say 'no';*
3  *The courage to govern.*

In the following sections, I will detail what this means and why these represent critical elements in bringing meaning into a corporation's innovation engagements, and why we sometimes need to do things that can seem contradictory in order to build courageous cultures.

## The courage to allow

One of my great heroes of all time is 'Amazing' Grace Hopper, one of the true pioneers of programming and an all-round badass. She created the first compiling tools, was a key figure in the development of COBOL (the first real programming language for business use), and at 79 still served as a rear admiral in the Navy. If that wasn't enough, she also had a quick wit, proven not least by her brilliant maxim: *'It's easier to ask forgiveness than it is to get permission'*. This seems to also have been something of a life philosophy and one that seems to have defined the deep innovation culture of early computing.

The reason I bring this up here is because the act of courage that managers seem to struggle with the most is this: the practice of allowing people to act without explicit permission. Even though we've long known that a feeling of being empowered is critical in engagement, motivation and the desire to enact change, many managers still struggle with letting go of the command-and-control logics of yesteryear. Whilst most companies talk a good game when it comes to delegation and empowerment, the fact is that most still react badly if an employee takes matters into their own hands. The result of this will usually be a dressing down, in private or in public, teaching the employee not to think that innovation actually means doing something new.

The best innovation leaders go beyond this. We've all heard of companies where employees can utilize an agreed budget to set things right if a customer complains, or where employees can use a specified amount of their working time for their own projects. These are good things, but the true test of just how bold an organization is lies in how it reacts when an employee has truly 'left the reservation' in pursuit of an innovation. Will you, as a manager, punish an employee for taking an unauthorized risk, or will you use this as a positive example? How will you cast questions of permission and forgiveness?

There have of course been many innovators who've walked the fine line between the acceptable and the fraudulent in the pursuit of the new. Richard Branson has encouraged and nurtured an image of being a rule-breaker and a maverick, and Thomas Alva Edison was famously unconcerned with the finer details of ethics and law in his strive to build an empire of innovation. However, many organizations still struggle when an employee shows a similar freewheeling attitude. In one of the companies I studied, the CEO adopted a rather creative approach to this.

I saw this when giving a keynote speech at their internal conference, where I upon arrival was told the CEO had decreed that my speech was to be postponed slightly to make space for an employee to 'explain himself' in front of all the managers of the company. He had run a project that had taken some liberties with budgets and the like, and that in the end had failed, and this was what he was asked to talk on. He was less than thrilled about this, a sentiment I wholeheartedly shared, particularly as I really didn't want this as the 'warm-up act' to my keynote speech. Still, the CEO was adamant. The speech was not a pleasant experience. The employee, Bob (not his real name), stammered, hemmed and hawed. The audience sat through his presentation with the pained silence of fellow sufferers. And then the CEO took to the stage.

He marched on, confidently, and didn't even walk up to Bob, who by now looked like he might faint. Instead, he pointed at him. Then he intoned 'I hate losing money'. The room was quiet as a mausoleum with particularly good soundproofing. The CEO turned around and addressing his managers, shouted 'but what I hate more is that there aren't more people here with the guts and the hearts of this man'. He went on to detail the promotion and bonus he had in store for Bob, to the whoops and cheers of the audience. Well, everyone except me. Let me tell you, it's difficult to follow that.

The reason I tell this story is that this so clearly highlights the courage to allow. The courage to see a rule breaker, and one who has failed at that, and still decide that this is worthy of praise. These are the kinds of leadership actions that instil courage in organizations and make people believe that top management means what they say when they encourage people to take risks and innovate.

## The courage to say 'no'

If instilling a courageous culture was as easy as simply rewarding rule-breaking, everyone would be doing it. Obviously, managers need to be careful walking the tightrope between productive risk-taking and careless waste of resources. This gets further complicated by the fact that as paradoxical as it may seem, sometimes the most courageous thing you can do with regards to innovation is to say no to it. I've already addressed the need to say no to the kind of superficial and shallow nonsense that permeates much of the innovation industry, but sometimes this needs to be extended to innovation in general. Now, if there is one thing that innovation pundits tend to agree on, it is some variation of this: 'Innovation should be a normal, everyday occurrence in the organization, part of its day-to-day business'. Too bad that this is a fantasy, and sometimes a dangerous one.

The reason innovation is powerful lies specifically in the fact that it breaks with the common state of affairs. Just like having a drink or a greasy burger is so much more delightful and fulfilling when they are not daily affairs (I won't judge you if they are), so innovation is most powerful when it hasn't been turned into a routine and a continuous slog. That said, many executives seem to think that innovation should be turned into the kind of repetitive affair many feel their work already is. The dangers inherent in such a view has often been downplayed or downright ignored. This notwithstanding, a central part of the contemporary plague of innovation fatigue is the inability of modern managers to delineate business as usual from innovation. The former requires a quantum of control and a modicum of predictability, whilst the latter needs to distance itself from both. Sadly, this fundamental tension is not recognized enough.

Companies that choose to ignore the contradiction between the smooth running of a business and the disruption of constant innovation, will quickly find themselves in a situation where the differing demands these two dynamics have confuse and confound the organization. Should you ignore or embrace your core competencies? Are experience and connections good or bad things? As most top managers know, the answer to such questions is 'yes' and 'both', but management thinking isn't designed to deal with such complexity.

## Innovation is a sometime thing

One of the most amazing executives I've ever known was the CEO of a company that made machinery for extractive industries. The company excelled in delivering high-quality technologies to their clients, but their clients communicated that their innovativeness left something to be desired (a point of view the board seemed to share). The CEO was a relatively new hire and noted that he was actually the second top executive who'd been brought in to make the company more innovative. His predecessor had been quite active in this space and had started a number of initiatives. Many of these had floundered, however, and a quick analysis showed that the projects lacked adequate resources, primarily due to the fact that there were so many innovation projects that it was difficult for people to find time for them all. In our conversations, the CEO said that whilst he didn't have the word for it at the time, his organization was suffering from severe innovation fatigue.

In a move that surprised practically everyone, the CEO's reaction to this was to declare a company-wide moratorium on innovation. Yes, you read that correctly. He stated, through emails and an all-hands meeting, that the company would put a temporary pause on all innovation activities. Ideas were not explicitly forbidden, but people were asked to note them and save them for later. Now, the CEO stated, focus would be on the daily business and the daily business only. Unsurprisingly, this met with some resistance. Some of the more enthusiastic innovation advocates in the company accused the CEO of trying to kill the company, and according to his own statements, the board voiced similar concerns. Despite this, the new leader persisted. For a set number of months, innovation would in effect be frozen, to be followed by a period during which innovation would be a key strategic focus.

Surprisingly for some, and unsurprisingly for me, this radical move ended up *improving* the overall innovation climate in the organization. Despite the murmurings of some innovation enthusiasts, the majority of the organization was happy to get some respite from the relentless pressure of multiple and sometimes overlapping innovation initiatives. The extra time the moratorium afforded helped deal with piled-up issues and full inboxes. Meetings improved, as they didn't always need to connect to innovation projects. As people got on top of their basic tasks, job enjoyment increased.

Whilst the moratorium was in effect, there was little innovation going on. At least not openly. What was interesting to note, however, was that once the moratorium ended, and the CEO announced that innovation projects could and should be started anew, the energy in the organization had transformed. People rejoined innovation teams willingly. Managers stated that the project teams all seemed energized and that the level of ideas had improved. It also became clear that people had been documenting new ideas continuously during the moratorium and were now eager to share them. The reasons should be obvious. Just as in any other human activity, a break from something can be an excellent thing to make it both more exciting and increase your enjoyment of it. No matter if it is burgers, booze or innovation.

*Sometimes the most daring thing an organization can do is to say 'no' to innovation itself!*

*Sometimes, then, the most daring thing an organization can do is to say 'no' to innovation itself!* Saying 'no' to innovation, not completely, not for all time, but so that innovation remains something special and meaningful, not a constant demand and pressure that only facilitates fatigue, may be the most daring thing an organization can do. In fact, with the otherwise relentless talk about innovation often killing the thing it praises, taking a break from it all and saying no to 'innovation as usual' might be the most courageous thing a manager can do.

## The courage to govern

Having noted the courage to allow and the courage to say no, we also need to acknowledge that the responsibility to craft a courageous culture doesn't sit with top management alone. We've already touched upon how every member of an organization should take at least a modicum of responsibility (to speak up, if nothing else) for an innovation culture. But what about those who are not fully outside, yet not fully inside? I here refer to boards of directors and advisory boards. These are critical parts of the wider governance structure of a corporation that are too often left out when discussing innovation and the organizational culture that supports it (or fails to do so).

A study conducted by Groysberg, Cheng and Bell surveyed 5,000 corporate board members all over the globe.[15] From an innovation governance perspective, the findings were rather depressing. A mere 30 per cent saw that innovation was a key issue, and a scant 21 per cent saw technological change as a major strategic challenge. In fact, when ranking strategic challenges, innovation is just barely in the top five. This indicates boards think that their companies are already on top of such matters, which stands in stark contrast to the already mentioned figure of 94 per cent of CEOs being displeased with the results of their investments into innovation.

What we're faced with, then, is that in order to establish a truly courageous culture, one where innovation is something more than an expected set of supplications, the entire governance structure of a corporation needs to be involved. The courage to govern for innovation is not merely one of being part of a governing body but realizing just how deeply notions of risk and responsibility need to be established. It would be easy to make the courage of allowing experiments just a trick, a way to manipulate sentiment in an organization. The courage to say no can be turned into a trick as well, a superficial set of contrarian moves. For courage to be truly embedded into an organization, there needs to be a daring structure of governance, one that transcends just checking the KPIs.

Still, boards of directors are often established in a way that minimizes this. Directors are routinely picked not for their bold ideas but for their experience and thus for their learnt practices. This can, in the worst-case scenario, make the board – the instance that is meant to encourage forward-thinking approaches and a strategic outlook – an institution that puts profits before purpose, money before meaning. If this is the case, if the board of directors isn't connected to and engaged in the establishment of a culture of deep innovation, then there is a distinct risk that this will adversely affect the way in which members of the organization view attempts to engage the culture. A courageous culture needs support, and a fearful and overly careful governance structure can fundamentally affect how meaningful the members of the organization feel the innovation efforts are.

I wish that I could say that most of the boards I've worked with were courageous and bold, but that would be a lie. I have worked with some that are, but most have been designed to spot errors rather than opportunities, follow the metrics of yesteryear rather than give chances to the things we might measure next year. This isn't necessarily the fault of the directors, as they have been selected and set up to do precisely this. Rather it is the fault of those tasked with establishing governance structures, who have failed to ensure that this is done in a way that brings courage to the organization and meaning to their innovation aspirations.

## The fifth R: resilience

The three forms of courage listed earlier are of course not enough, but they are important building blocks of an organization that can weather the winds of change. We live in turbulent times. New technologies are introduced at bewildering speeds, and the world of global politics has become not just volatile but chaotic. Consumer behaviour changes, institutions that used to be the bedrock of society are falling apart and new ones emerge seemingly overnight. No wonder, then, that many business gurus state that companies need to become agile, flexible, ambidextrous, fluid. Many are the CEOs I've talked with who have expressed a desire that their organizations could be organized and reorganized at will, rapidly evolving and mutating to face whatever happens to be thrown at them next.

This, however, is only part of the puzzle. Whilst flexibility and adaptability are fine things to wish for in an organization, they are not sufficient. An organization that is perfectly adaptable is much like a band of mercenaries, prepared to fight any war as long as the pay is good and the munitions are there. Such an organization can be very successful in the short run, even in the medium run if the environment is right, but just like you can't use mercenaries to build a nation, you can't create a great company just by adapting to any- and everything. Instead, a company that aims for something more than a quick buck needs to develop resilience.

Resilience, as I use it here, refers to that core of purpose and identity that enables an organization to deal with adversity and changing conditions, and even to transcend the faddish changes in their environment.[16] The reason I speak here of finding a purpose and to translate that into a series of meaningful engagements, is because too much of the debate on innovation deals with trying to please whatever faddish desire exists in the market.

Companies with deep innovation cultures are resilient not because they've found a magic bean of innovation but because they know why they attempt to innovate, what connection this has to the purpose of the organization and what can be disregarded because it is shallow, crowd-pleasing, PR-optimized corporate make-believe. To strengthen the resilience of your organization, then, is less an issue of becoming more 'innovative' and far more one of finding a purpose and rekindling ambition and courage in the same. The principles outlined in this chapter are part and parcel of this. By focusing on meaning and purpose, you make everyone in the company more attuned to why they do what they do and why that matters. By raising the level of ambition and introducing just the right amount of stress, you ensure that people are prepared to go the extra mile, even if there were to be bumps along the road. By emphasizing courage throughout the organization, including the courage to say no, you build willpower and grit.

Consider NASA, an agency that consistently has to fight for funding and which made the original moonshot. Tasked with a nigh-on impossible mission, they've nevertheless consistently shown an aptitude for solving incredibly difficult problems – including but not limited to adapting a $CO_2$ scrubber with duct tape, hose, socks and a bungee cord during the famous Apollo 13 mission. They are an organization with a clear purpose and a grand ambition, and thanks to these they have managed to remain consistently and unerringly innovative for far longer than most 'innovative organizations' have existed. They are the epitome of a resilient innovation culture, a culture that combines a deeply meaningful purpose that allows for them to think in years and decades (and thus transcend shallow notions of innovation) as well as improvise on the spot when this is required. By being something more than simply innovation for the sake of innovation, they have been a beacon of deep innovation for decades and have inspired generations.

The example of NASA serves as a perfect bridge from notions of purpose, ambition and courage to our next chapter. Founded in 1968, but with a prehistory that goes back to 1915 (and the National Advisory Committee for Aeronautics), it is still a core innovation agency. A manifold of innovations, such as LASIK eye surgery, freeze drying food, digital image sensors in phones and other cameras, and modern solar cells (and many, many things besides) can all be traced back to NASA projects. Courageous and ambitious, it has shown that some innovation takes decades and that some innovation thinking needs to be considered in centuries, yet it has also shown a remarkable ability to improvise and think on its feet. It is this, the diversity of innovation times and tempos to which we will turn in our penultimate chapter.

# CHAPTER SEVEN

# Time, velocity, slack

## Working at the speed of innovation

*'Oh my ears and whiskers, how late it's getting!'*
LEWIS CARROLL

## Working on innovation time

Innovation takes time. I know… Shocking, right? Still this very trivial fact contains a surprising amount of depth, with strange assumptions and ignored truths often skewing the manner in which we understand innovation time. In this chapter, we will inquire into the many times (plural!) of innovation and why an understanding of temporal diversity can promote healthy innovation cultures. Innovation doesn't have one time, but rather dances to a multitude of beats, tempos, rhythms. Sometimes, innovation is defined by the staccato and the insistent beats of a boisterous rap. At other times, it is defined by the languorous and sorrowful sound of a sad country song. And yet, both are attuned to innovation time.

Innovation is often talked of as if it were defined by speed, echoing the notion of dromology, or the science of speed, as this has been discussed by the philosopher Paul Virilio.[1] We speak of speed to market and of crunch time, and celebrate speedy slogans such as 'Move fast and break things!' (Now available as a poster, a coffee mug, a t-shirt, a hoodie, a pillow and a sticker from Startup Vitamins! This is not a joke and definitively not an advert. More a warning of an impending apocalypse.). This addiction notwithstanding, real innovation time is far more complex than the notion of relentless speed.

For a leader wishing to understand innovation, it is important that they understand innovation times as well. Run a project that requires a long gestation period like an agile sprint and you will end up with a project that doesn't live up to its potential. Run all experiments like they require years of patient testing and you'll end up with a mostly inert innovation culture with little agility or enthusiasm. We live in innovation times, and the plural form is important. Just like there are many kinds of ideas and many kinds of innovation, there are many kinds of times to all this.

## Between comfort and panic

The reason speed is so often seen as being at the heart of innovation is due to the energy that velocity brings. When people feel that there's energy and things happening, they are more likely to accept novel ideas, agree to experiments, accept odd new ways of doing things. Further, when people feel that there is no immediate need to change things, they can get lethargic, comfortable, slow. In other words, innovation often requires a change of tempo, a shift in the rhythms of an organization. Sometimes this shift might be something small, such as reacting in a curious, nurturing way to ideas, getting a conversation rolling. At other times, it might be a question of making people aware of a crisis they've previously been ignoring.

I've found it difficult to trace the true background of using 'burning platform' as a metaphor for necessary change in an organization. Some things seem clear, however. In July 1988, an oil-drilling platform named Piper Alpha suffered a catastrophic fire, killing 168 people. Only 63 crew-members survived, some by simply jumping off the burning platform into the ice-cold North Sea. This disaster was broadly publicized in media, and the notion of jumping off a burning platform started to get used in organizational change. The term became world known, however, thanks to an internal memo at Nokia. CEO Stephen Elop might not have turned the company around, but his message about just how difficult the situation was for the once mighty mobile communications company made headline news. By describing Nokia as a burning platform,[2] and by thus drawing a parallel between it and a deadly disaster in the making, he certainly shook the organizational culture and cemented the place of the term in the broader business lexicon.

Today, when we refer to a burning platform, we're in effect saying that business as usual will kill us. In such a situation, it matters less exactly what we do and more that we start doing something. When a CEO declares the company to be in this kind of a position, this is done to make everyone understand that there is a qualitative difference between then and now. Time has shifted, in such a telling, and the old rules no longer apply. This kind of declaration, in which a state of exception is invoked, can be a very powerful thing. If we look at major turn-around efforts, we can often find that they hinged on there being a moment in which management openly stated that the company could go down in flames. Nothing like imminent death to focus the mind.

This said, you can really only do this once. When you ring this kind of alarm bell, effectively signalling that there's been a rift in time and that exceptional measures are being taken, you can create a sense of urgency and make people more inclined to innovate. However, once this is done, it is exceedingly difficult to do it again (at least unless several years have passed). Just like the boy who cried wolf, people will tire of the manager who cries crisis. You cannot invoke endless velocity and constantly demand more, as this only creates fatigue. Worse than that, it can make talk of crises and the need for radical new ways of working sound like just so much hot air.

The smart manager realizes that yes, talking of a burning platform is one way to work with innovation time. But it is only one and a particularly unique one at that. *We might talk of innovation management as having a toolbox of different times.* The chaotic energy created by invoking a metaphor such as the burning platform comes from one such time, but there are many others besides – so many I could write a book on them alone. In the following sections I will just outline some of these and the varying ways in which these innovation times work and the direct effect they have on innovation cultures. The times I'll primarily focus on are:

1  *the rapid times of agile spurts;*
2  *brief, powerful moments in time;*
3  *slow, patient times;*
4  *pauses and breaks.*

I will also touch upon notions such as tempo and slack, and end with a call for managers who wish to work with innovation to see time not as an objective, given thing, but as something that can be played with in imaginative ways.

## Agile spurts

Whilst it is not true that all innovation is fast, the thing most people associate with innovation projects is rapid development. Here, innovation time is something akin to a smaller, less extreme version of invoking a crisis. It still represents a break with the often languid, structured time of business as usual but in a way that emphasizes that this is a time-limited break. The quick spurt has a beginning and an end, and many a manager has been able to inject energy into their organizations by having it deal with quick deadlines. Agile methods, originally introduced in the software industry but increasingly deployed everywhere, represent a version of this, a reworking of how we view development time.

The logic of agile development – which may at times be called lean, or scrum, or experimental, or just 'startup-like' – is that it emphasizes quick bursts of activity and continuous follow ups. Rather than attempting a well-structured plan and timeline, agile methods (by any other name – you'll find that the evangelists for each of the loosely coupled methods are orthodox about how their method is both better and totally different from all the seemingly similar ones...) emphasize quick hacks and continuous improvement. You work on a new project for a set amount of time, such as a week or 14 days, constantly reviewing and reassessing.

The reason such moves can work is that they change assumptions and the way an organization views time. If you're expected to do something in seven days, rather than seven weeks or months, your levels of ambition change. You have less time to second-guess yourself, and you'll be more likely to try out more unorthodox ideas as you have less to lose. The power of compressed times is that they manage to make organizations more action focused, whilst at the same time lessening the cost of experimentation. If you fail, there's always next week. This is also why hackathons work, as they do the same in 24–48 hours, effectively forcing participants into execution rather than evaluation.

This is of course not to say that forcing the organization into agile spurts will automatically make it more innovative. If made into a repetitive process, agile spurts can bore and fatigue the organization just like a slow stage-gate model can. Further, not all kinds of innovations suit such methods – as my friends at Boeing might say, some parts of aeronautics' developments just have to take the time they take. That said, the shift in planning horizon that agile methods introduce can be very energizing for a corporation, particularly if this marks a clear shift from how things used to be done.

It can also free up some surprising elements of a corporation's cognitive surplus. In my work with a medium-sized technology company, one that had previously been empathetic about the need to have extremely stringent and safety-focused processes, a small test produced surprising results. The company's development processes had usually been measured in quarters, so that three months was a quite common project stage length. Projects were always headed by seasoned experts and rarely involved members of the organization without deep technical expertise. As a result, fewer than 20 per cent of the organization in a survey stated that they were 'engaged' or 'very engaged' in the company's innovation endeavours. Top management was less than happy with this result and wanted to test out alternative models, even though many of the experts considered this a waste of time.

As an experiment, the company ran a project in which teams comprised of people from all parts of the organization were asked to run quick development programmes. These ran in parallel to the already established innovation projects, but differed in that once every two weeks the groups presented their progress so far. The project gave rise to quite a number of tests and trials, out of which not all those many went on to be actualized innovations. This might seem like a failed experiment, but the real results could be found elsewhere. After six months, when the organization was once again surveyed, the amount of people who stated they were engaged or very engaged with innovation in the company had more than doubled – a figure made even more interesting by the fact that the number of people engaged in the agile experiments was less than the rise in engagement. In other words, even people who had not taken part in this rapid innovation time felt a higher degree of engagement! In addition, the experiment did give rise to at least two projects that went onto the 'real' innovation programme of the company.

What the project did, in essence, was it showed the organization that not all innovation work had to be the long, stringent and expert-led projects they'd been used to. Instead, this faster way of working allowed for alternative forms of engagement, serving as a kind of 'softer' arena for innovation. Many other organizations have further found that an engagement with agile methodologies (by any other name) can even supplant some of the more slow-moving ways of developing.

In other words, if you feel that your company's innovation times are too slow and languid, switch things around. Set rapid deadlines, emphasizing smaller steps forward, but more of them. Make the culture take responsibility for taking part in innovation, even if it is in a more piecemeal fashion. The new kind of innovation time can reward you with both a path to test out ideas that might not fit with your current innovation management processes and increase overall engagement with ideas. Both are a good thing. Over time and in the moment.

## The importance of moments

In an organization, every moment can be a moment of innovation. Obviously not so that every moment can engender a disruptive or radical innovation, but still so that every moment can be made 'innovation meaningful'. For leaders, this means that they need to be aware both of how ideas can be killed through a moment's micro-aggression and also of how one can build a stronger, happier, more energized culture by being prepared to act with purpose when the moment arises.

In *The Culture Code*, Daniel Coyle details how high-performing and successful teams are often defined by the manner in which they establish a base level of safety (psychological and otherwise), share vulnerability (i.e. reflect on things that may have gone wrong) and establish purpose.[3] All of these themes take a long time to establish, but what is more interesting is that they are built not through major projects and showy events but through small gestures and cues that signal belonging and safety. This might be simply affirmations repeated in the morning (or evening, if that's more your style), or the conscious choice of leaders to look out for meaningful moments when such cues might best be deployed.

One of the great mysteries of innovation leadership has to be the fact that many wannabe leaders fail to utilize the very simplest of idea-supporting behaviours. A very successful CEO I once met one who ran a company with a very good track-record for sustained innovation, described this beautifully when he said his great 'secret' for innovation was... pointing. He said (and I'm paraphrasing, as we were in a bar and I didn't record the conversation): 'Big words only confuse people. They confuse me too. I like to focus on the simple act of whenever someone presents or does something great, I point and go "This! This is what I want to see more of!" There's nothing as powerful as an easily graspable example'.

He had spotted a very important truth about building culture. Without clear examples, delivered in the moment, we often tend to pontificate in generalities. Whilst this might make for impressive after-dinner speaking, it doesn't build healthy and lively cultures. Far more important might be to actually act in the moment and clarify your vision through a series of visible, clear examples. Chip and Dan Heath, in their book *The Power of Moments*,[4] have forcefully argued for paying attention to small moments through which you can convey a core message about your vision and your purpose. Rather than focusing on the big picture, you might in fact do much better by looking to the fleeting moments in which you can give a condensed lesson about the things you wish to enhance, support and duplicate.

It is one thing to state a general notion about wanting to support risk-taking in your company. It is a completely different one to ensure that you have a Bob on stage (remember him, from Chapter 6?) and create a moment to remember. It is easy to say that you want to support challenging projects and a completely different (and often more difficult) thing to stop everything in a meeting or at a conference, point, and say 'This, this is what I think we should be doing!'

Every company has a plethora of moments, all day and every day, during which a leader can set an example. Most moments are lost to time because leaders do not act on them. What my CEO friend tried to point out was that each and every one of these offers us the chance to point and say 'This!' Some of these moments are funny, others are emotional. Some of them come at a critical juncture for the company, whereas others are far more mundane. What is important about all of them, however, is that they can be used by leaders to strengthen the innovation culture and clarify what innovation could and should mean in the organization.

*Every company has a plethora of moments, all day and every day, during which a leader can set an example.*

Innovation time isn't just about speed or slowness. It's not just about process and projects. Sometimes innovation is at its most visible when there is a moment when it can be highlighted, turned into an example, pointed to. Sometimes you need to build these moments, such as when you flunk something on purpose to show the organization that it is OK to fail. Sometimes you may need to make yourself look silly, so that the organization can connect to its own imagination – let me just say that I've seen leaders do unconvincing drag performances just to introduce their organizations to the joys of failure. Cultures are by nature long-term things, but they are often made up of meaning-ful, playful, reflective moments.

## Long slogs

In our social imagination, there is a picture of the innovator as an impatient, twitchy, action-oriented man (yeah, I wrote man, and I meant it – reread Chapter 5). For this imagined innovator, there's nothing worse than the slow churn of the regular organi-zation, and we view him as the very enemy of the mind-numbing slow slog of non-disruptive, careful, thoughtful action. Which just goes to show how badly the innovation industry has managed to poison our general thinking regarding how revolu-tions happen.

*If there is one thing that is required of leaders of innovative organizations, it is patience.* Whilst the innovation literature

*If there is one thing that is required of leaders of innovative organizations, it is patience.*

often wants to imply that innovations can be created in no time at all, the reality is that many if not most innovations require a very long time to gestate, develop and bloom. The research into packet switching that marks the start of the internet was initiated in the early 1960s. The precursor to the internet, ARPANET, was rocking a full 15 sites in late 1971. In 1982, we had a standard for the Internet Protocol Suite (TCP/IP). After this, it only took a decade to create a commercial opportunity for early adopters. A decade after this, in 2002, we had almost 10 per cent of the world population connected. Or, to put it in another way, it was an instant success 40 to 50 years in the making.

Now, imagine you have an employee that comes to you and says, 'I'd like a million dollars to explore a technology, that might be really important 40 years from now'. Would you sign off on it? Yes, I know it's a trick question. We all like to imagine that we would, but the reality is that 99.97 per cent of people who make this kind of request are more or less kindly asked to go away. Of the remaining 0.03 per cent, most are fired. A very few might be given a chance, but they are too few to properly consider. Our systems are simply not built to consider long-term projects, nor designed to exhibit patience.

This is a problem, for as the World Economic Forum has stated, what the world needs is *patient capital*.[5] Particularly when we talk of major, world-changing innovations, the development paths may well be many decades long – as for instance the case with GPS (shoutout to Hedy Lamarr) shows. If investment and support flows only to projects that promise a payout in months, we will miss out on or delay more transformative innovations. For companies, which often think in short time periods, the very notion of thinking in years can at times sound like an impossibility. Then again, they've never considered Chester Carlson.

You've probably never heard of Carlson, but you've most certainly used his innovation. He is the genius behind xerography, today better known as dry photocopying. He got the original patent for this – US Patent 2,297,691 – in 1942. A scant 17 years later, this patent was at the heart of the Xerox 914, famous as 'the most successful single product of all time'. One of the other architects of the product, John Dessauer, has been referred to as a key resource in turning a company with a turnover in the low millions into a multi-billion dollar behemoth. Even taking the two decades of development into the equation, that's pretty impressive. Still, this is not the kind of story that the innovation industry admires. It is too slow, too fraught with challenges.

But what would you pay to have a Chester Carlson in your company? Someone who has an off-the-wall idea, one that might take over a decade to turn into a commercially viable product but which might make your company not 10 times bigger, not 100 times bigger, but 1,000 times bigger? Carlson makes Google's desire for projects to be 10× or 100× seem positively quaint. Xerox might have been lucky, but they also taught us a valuable lesson – sometimes innovation times are very slow indeed.

The lesson for managers here is clear: beware of quick pay-offs. Whilst this example might be extreme in both duration and pay-off, the logic still holds. Some innovations require far more time than others. A sensible manager will try to have agile and rapid innovation processes in play but also allow for far slower, more fundamental innovation shifts. The long slog is more diffi-cult to deal with than the agile spurt, but that does not mean it is any less impactful. You might think that attuning your mind to innovation time means that you need to insist on fast results and faster pivots, but the reality is that sometimes the opposite is required.

Do you have a strategy in place for radical patience? Is your company prepared to do bets that may take a decade to play out? Are you comfortable with betting on both projects that might pay out in months and those that will necessarily require years of development money? An innovation leader that only focuses on the quick payback is not a leader. The culture that only supports fast-sprouting seeds is flawed. Yes, there is much to admire in speed-of-light innovation, but this does not mean that this is all there is. After all, sometimes the fastest way to innovate is to not innovate at all...

## Power pauses: why we need time off from innovation

Towards the end of Chapter 6, we discussed the odd case of the CEO who introduced a moratorium on innovation. I would like to return to this here, as we need to consider non-time, or the stopping of time, as a perfectly valid way to deal with innovation in corporations. No matter if we're talking about speedy or slow approaches to innovation, both work from the assumption that there needs to be active innovation projects in a company. Whilst this might seem self-evident to people brainwashed by the innovation industry, this is a dangerous assumption. Sometimes, the best way to encourage innovation in an organization is to utterly disregard it.

With all things in life, it is difference and juxtaposition that create energy. In an organization with nothing but engineers, a single philosopher or designer can create tremendous energy. In an organization that has always treated innovation as a multi-year process, agile methods make a difference. It matters not what kind of innovation times you wish for; it is the capacity to introduce a new rhythm that increases innovation dynamics. Part of introducing new rhythms is the deployment of pauses and silences. Miles Davis, the genius who revolutionized the art form of jazz not once, not twice, but three times – hard bop, cool jazz and jazz fusion (and I'm not even mentioning the genius that is *Sketches of Spain* here) – told his band 'Don't play what's there; play what's not there'. He had a deep understanding of novelty and the manner in which not playing a note could be so much more than playing it. It is not until you've encouraged people to take strategic breaks and utilize strategic silences that you've enlisted the full gamut of smart innovation moves…

The reason a pause or a break works is because it somewhat paradoxically creates both calm and tension. It creates a space of calm because it creates a distance to what has occurred before and allows a person to disengage. At the same time, a pause builds tension, as we often do not know how long the break or pause will go on for. In organizations, such as in the case alluded to earlier, a pause also does double duty. On the one hand, a break from innovation allows for people to take care of other things, without feeling guilty about not being all 'innovate or die'. This is energizing, as it lessens innovation fatigue and stress but also because it allows for focusing on different things. On the other hand, a break from innovation will make the break from the break, i.e. starting up innovation activities again, so much more meaningful. When innovation is no longer a constant demand from the organization, people can start to reconnect with what it means for them and how ideas can be realized in the organizations.

In Chapter 3, whilst discussing the role of responsibility in an innovation culture, I detailed some work I did with a Danish company – work that involved making innovation projects non-mandatory. In essence, that story detailed what happened when people were allowed to choose whether or not to partake in various innovation working groups, in effect being given the power to pause their engagement. Interestingly, the very fact that they were given this opportunity often meant that employees in the firm first opted out of innovation, only to return in a more energized way later down the line. This shouldn't surprise us, of course, as we all know how a holiday or even a weekend can energize us greatly. Yet many companies insist on endless iterations of innovation talk and initiatives, without once considering the costs of this.

My old supervisor, professor Claes Gustafsson, even coined a word for such energies. Whereas everyone knows synergy, when two systems are combined and generate more energy or dynamism than they did separately, few have heard of *idiergy*. This is the energy created by separation, pauses, splits. It can emerge when a lethargic company is split into several smaller, more energetic ones. Semiconductors, the building blocks of our modern world, essentially function by mixing conductive and non-conductive matter in creative ways, introducing an idiergetic break. A monotone mono-tone becomes music by the introduction of pauses and breaks, and a tired innovation culture can, at times, be revived simply by introducing a moment to take a break and catch your breath. This is the power of idiergy, and a manager in a fatigued organization can create miraculous things by utilizing it intelligently.

## Designing for slack

Another reason why pauses are important for innovation lies in the very nature of creativity itself. For as long as we've researched creativity, we've known that ideas often emerge in the in-between times, the times not necessarily occupied with busywork. We often get our best ideas in spaces not normally seen as innovation spaces – walks in the park, that moment just before you fall asleep and, as is always mentioned, showers. Some creativity consultants of my acquaintance have even gone so far as to suggest always having a notebook with you to capture the ideas generated in these places far from the madding work crowds. And, I imagine, a whiteboard for your shower stall.

In-between times are powerful due to the makeup of the creative mind. When working on a problem, we often do much of this work subconsciously. During the times we are focused on the problem, the subconscious rarely engages with it, but when we let this focus go, the subconscious can kick in. The power inherent in this is hard to overestimate. This is when our mind goes into a kind of imaginative dream state, sifting through a mass of inputs, experiences, sensations and whatever might flow through our mind. Subconsciously we combine things that cannot be combined, test out variations that make no sense, much like in a dream. Often this gives rise to silly combinations, implausible or irrational notions, but every so often something arises out of this mad jumble of inputs that actually is a partially formed answer to the problem we've been working with, at which point the conscious mind is re-engaged.

The moment (see what I did there?) this happens can feel not unlike being hit with a ball in the back of the head. Some call it a flash of insight. We're walking along in a forest, and suddenly we see a solution that seems utterly sensible, yet we have no idea where it came from. We just know. What really happened when we took a break was that our mind could engage in imaginative play, and our conscious mind could pick a working idea out of the primordial ooze of our subconscious. The slack we allowed for our brain kicked in another kind of thinking, a more imaginative kind, and as a result a new idea emerged.

On an individual level we all understand this, as we've experienced it. But how do you build in this kind of slack, this kind of time for the unconscious mind to operate, into your organization and its culture? For executives, there's always the opportunity to simply take breaks and ask a secretary to hold all calls. For freelancers, undisturbed walks in the park (or a sneaky drink in the middle of the day) are self-evident perks. But for most people in the organization this isn't necessarily allowed. Increasingly we see that people are simply asked to work longer, take shorter breaks, attend more meetings and answer more messages on email, Slack and social media. And after all this, some managers still ask why the people in their organization aren't more innovative!

***An organization that wants to be innovative needs to design for slack***. The organization needs to break out of a mindset in which slack equals waste and inefficiency, and realize that without space to think imaginatively, an organization in effect wastes the cognitive surplus it desperately needs to compete in today's economy. To design for slack is not the same as giving everyone time to amble aimlessly in a suitable nearby forest. Neither is it a question of building in inefficiencies. Instead it is the art of thinking strategically about how an organization can support performance. Here, initiatives such as capping overtime and discouraging emails (and answering them) outside office hours have consistently been proved to improve efficiency rather than limit it. Some organizations go so far as to actively encourage napping, amongst them *Huffington Post* and (annoyingly enough for me) Google.[6] Similarly, I've often encouraged organizations to experiment with fewer and shorter meetings in order to give the culture some much

*An organization that wants to be innovative needs to design for slack.*

needed slack. What it all comes down to is that we need to realize that innovation isn't just about harder, faster, stronger, more. If anything, it is about appreciating all the tempos and the rhythms of the organization.

## Shifting rhythms and the rough patches

Almost every innovation project reaches a point at which everything seems to slow down. These are times when resistance, external or internal, seems to make things crawl, and they can be very trying for those who are invested in the innovation in question. We are often acutely aware of slowing down as a phenomenon, even more so than we are to things speeding up. I mention this here because in much of what I've written about in this book, the assumption has been that projects are either fast or slow, when in reality they can often shift through a wide range of velocities.

This is something that you can come across particularly in basic research, where breakthroughs can be few and far between, but where one can well engender several others in rapid succession. Initially, the group may have wrestled with a tough science problem, testing several forms of attachments that in the end turn out to be dead ends. Seasoned researchers know that this is nigh-on inevitable and will not be discouraged. It can be a draining process, however, particularly if it goes on for a longer period. Then, for whatever reason, a breakthrough appears. Everyone is overjoyed, as the work put in now feels meaningful. This energy can sometimes lead to a situation where either due to the breakthrough or due to the energy in the group, several other successes follow. The group feels as if it is zooming ahead, flying, invincible. Then... nothing. For whatever reason, the next big thing doesn't appear. The breakthrough starts to feel like yesterday's news, and the feelings of greatness get supplanted by feelings of guilt.

Those times when an innovation project hits a rough, slow patch can be difficult ones for leaders and companies (and I've seen something quite similar play out in everything from business model innovation to new product launches). Whereas a sudden lurch forwards requires little more than a modicum of governance, so that things aren't forgotten as the group is caught in the creative process, slowing down requires much more. Most of all, it requires that leaders do not start demanding the impossible of the group. Companies that experience an innovation slowdown often react as if in a panic, insisting that what the situation requires is more focus on innovation, more demands, more stress. In reality, what the group or the company requires might well be the opposite.

Innovation, as a dynamic in human creation, isn't relentless progress at constant speed. It isn't an inexorable march, at least not one without variation and fluctuation. Instead, it is like all other human activity, something that progresses at many paces, many rhythms.

## Human, all too human rhythms

*What we've discussed here so far might be summarized as a culture of deep innovation that is in tune with its own rhythms.*

*What we've discussed might be summarized as a culture of deep innovation that is in tune with its own rhythms.*

A culture of deep innovation mixes up speedy spurts with patient projects, takes a break when a break is needed and increases the tempo when the moment is just right. Leading an innovative organization can thus metaphorically be likened to being a conductor. It is to allow for the slow movements and to work up to the occasional fortissimo. It is to create a rhythm but also to understand that this cannot just be a driving, constant beat. It is to have a deep understanding for what people need to feel cared for and safe, and what is required for people to be able to engage with their imagination.

Great innovation leaders thus spend considerable time trying to understand both the people in the organization and the manner in which the culture makes sense of the varied time of innovation. This is rarely a straight-forward process. In many of the companies I've worked with, the sense of innovation time was quite different in different parts of the organization, and this difference tends to be particularly pronounced between the higher echelons of the hierarchy and the more operative parts. The top management team may well feel that the organization is slow, lethargic, unengaged with innovation, whilst the operative part talks of hectic schedules, the weeks being filled up with meetings, having no time to think and so on.

Understanding and respecting this is key to getting the culture onto its own working rhythms. Also, managers need to understand that here too, reciprocity is a key building block of a healthy innovation culture, capable of deep creativity. Without time to reflect and assess things, people will not be able to engage with innovation in a meaningful way. If you demand innovation, you need to create time for it. If you want to go fast, you may need to slow things down.

So, at times, the beat of innovation may well be rhythmic, but to truly lead also means being open to stranger alternatives. Syncopation, dissonance, bitonality, strange modalities. Sometimes slow and fast at the same time. Sometimes the other way around. This is why innovation is so difficult, almost… surreal. It can get on top of us, but in the end innovation is the work of humans, with all the strangeness that entails.

## The Kessel run: weird times in innovation

In *Star Wars*, the Kessel run is a hyperspace route that enables various kinds of smuggling and similar nefarious activities. Han Solo famously made it in slightly more than 12 parsecs, which curiously enough is a measure of distance rather than speed.

Here, this can stand as a metaphor for the difficulties of working in innovation time. Sometimes, a shortcut takes longer than the long way. Sometimes, speed slows you down. At other times, you can cut through space-time in a way that seems almost magical.

Successful innovation, particularly sustained successful innovation, is not unlike doing the Kessel run in 12 parsecs. It requires thinking creatively about time and space, sometimes bending both. It requires bending what we think is possible and ignoring those who would say something cannot be done. What is more, it requires that we let go of most of our notions of logic. Where some look only at time, or distance, or cost, the innovator realizes the fundamental relativity of all things. To innovate is often to bend the rules of physics and to recast notions of connectivity – to make the far apart close at hand and to make the dissimilar nigh identical.

If we look to the true innovative geniuses of all times, the Nikola Teslas and the Marie Curies, this was what drew people to them – their imaginative way of looking not only at the world but also at the manner in which their ideas seemed to transcend time and space. They, not unlike a later innovator who became endlessly eulogized by the innovation industry, created something like a 'reality distortion field', a space of ambition and vision that went beyond what people felt was possible.

In the end, this is what draws people to innovation. Not the riches, necessarily. Not the fancy stories about San Francisco. But the belief that we, too, if the time and place are right, can do the impossible. That sometimes an agile project can achieve what a long, sustained effort could not. Or that sometimes what looks slow and traditional can out-innovate the most speed-obsessed organization. Think back to Chester Carlson and modern photocopying, or the internet. Both innovations were decades in the making; both were steps that changed the world forever. One by starting to free women from mindless office drudgery,[7] the other by giving us hitherto unimagined capabilities to communicate and create. Both took a long time to get there, but once introduced, seemed to enable fantastic speeds and the folding together of time and space. A little like the Kessel run. And just like in the Kessel run, it's time for one more jump. This time to the final chapter.

# CHAPTER EIGHT

# Pulling it all together

## From 'innovation' to innovation

'*Innovations never happen as planned.*' GIFFORD PINCHOT

## On innovation pornography

A key product of the innovation industry is at the same time one of the most dangerous symptoms of shallow innovation: a form of innovation writing I've taken to calling ***innovation pornography***. This admittedly provocative term is my way of referring to the kind of glib and spurious presentations of innovation and innovative organizations that are the stock and trade of the innovation industry. This book has attempted to be an antidote to this, but to understand what I mean by all this it is necessary to first consider what pornography is, deep down.

Essentially, pornography is a cleaned up version of reality. This claim might confuse or even disturb some, who are used to thinking about porn as something dirty and disgusting. However, as obscene as it might at times be, pornography exists to tell simplified, polished stories about sex. This is because sex in the real world can be quite a messy, complicated thing. In the real world, people have hang-ups and headaches, not to mention busy schedules and children. None of this applies in pornography. In that make-believe world everyone and everything is beautiful. In other words, porn is utterly, gloriously unrealistic.

I'm not saying this to condemn pornography, nor the people who consume it. The problem occurs if you start believing that pornography is a true representation of reality and gets even worse if you live your life as if it were. Yet we often treat innovation in this way, and most of the stories in the innovation literature are presented in a distinctly pornographic manner.

## When we skip the messy bits

Reading a magazine like *Fast Company* or *Wired* is often quite exhilarating, with exciting stories and great pictures. So is going to a TED-talk, or listening to a famous innovation speaker, not to mention reading most books on innovation. In all of these, innovation is presented in pretty much the same way. Super-smart person gets a great idea. Some fuddy-duddies don't think it'll work, but quickly he (and yes, it's most often a he) finds like-minded people and gets support. The innovation gets introduced to the market, is joyously accepted by the customers and everyone is happy. All this is normally accompanied by slick photography and other visuals, and sometimes there is a soundtrack.

Now, if there is one thing I can say with total confidence, *that's not how innovation works*. Rather, innovation starts from some-one getting an idea, but not a great one. Half-baked would be a kind word to describe the first steps of an idea. Developing this idea will not be smooth but is often a messy affair. Some people will help, but sometimes the help makes things worse. Sometimes people try to kill the idea but inadvertently make it stronger. At some point, a prototype is developed, and not only does it look awful, but it looks nothing like the original idea. Sometimes everyone has forgotten what the idea initially was. This continues for some, with steps forwards, back, to the side, every which way but loose. Over the project, several crises, shouting matches, losses of faith and the occasional drunken binge will occur. When the innovation finally, somehow, gets to the market, many of the people who took part in the development have little to no idea how that happened. In short, it's a mess.

None of this tends to turn up in the magazines, the books, or the conference presentations. Sure, there might be an ever-so-humble self-deprecating reference thrown in for good measure, but these tend to be marginal. Innovation stories are written like fairy tales, but they're stage-set like pornography. All the fumbles, all the failures, all the confusion is swept aside. All that's left are a few carefully lighted scenes, curated so that everyone looks their best and the right climax is reached.

Now, this wouldn't be a problem unless some people actually believed in it. Just like pornography can be problematic if teen-agers see it and start believing that this is what healthy, normal sex looks like. *Innovation books are problematic only if you believe in them.*


## Pygmalion and the Golem in innovation

Now, the sad truth is that there are many managers out there who believe in innovation books, even the bad ones. This gives rise to many a problematic innovation behaviour, including judging your staff on how well they live up to the notions of what an innovation organization looks like by comparing it to the shallowness of 'innoporn'.

In education studies, a considerable amount of interest has been directed towards understanding the Pygmalion effect (sometimes alternately called the Rosenthal effect). This is an effect, originally studied by Robert Rosenthal and Lenore Jacobson,[1] where heightened expectations regarding the success and capabilities of students led to measurable increases in their performance. In other words, the Pygmalion effect states that if you believe students will do well, the likelihood that they will increases. The opposite of this is the Golem effect, which refers to the self-fulfilling prophecy that if you believe students will fail, the likelihood that they do increases. These effects have been widely studied, and owing to the psychological makeup of humans, they broadly hold true. Believe in people and they will excel. Doubt them and they will prove you right.

What innovation pornography does, is that it essentially heightens these effects in an organization. A leader who has been entranced by the latest shallow innovation book will be looking for specific behaviours and phenomena, and when not seeing these, treats the organization as if it were lacking. Similarly, a leader who is attuned to deep innovation and imagination will support the organization in fundamental ways. In the former case, the organization will become demoralized and consequently fulfil the image of being un-innovative. In the latter case, the trust and the respect the leader shows will lead to more innovative behaviours. No matter whether we believe our organization to be innovative or are convinced that it isn't, the Pygmalion/Golem effect will ensure that we are right. Not happy, necessarily, but right.

This is the insidious way in which the innovation industry damages innovation in our companies. By flogging a fallacious, reductionistic notion of innovation, it skews the minds of managers. By expecting the wrong things, at the wrong speeds, these can then do great damage to both budding ideas and emerging innovation cultures. You get the kind of innovation you ask for, and if what you ask for is the kind of fairy-tale innovation stories that ignore how the real world, and real people, work… Well, let's just say you shouldn't be surprised if there's no happy ending.

## After 'innovation': the return of the farmer

What this book has tried to argue for is an approach to innovation that emphasizes humility and care rather than living up to impossible expectations. In an organization where people are tired, bored and stressed by endless calls for more 'innovation', we need to find new ways of talking about it, new ways to criticize it, new ways to evaluate it. Where innovation pornography is more interested in showing off, we need to find a way back to innovation ambition. Where innovation pornography is all about surface and user interfaces, we need to find a way back to impact.

*Where innovation pornography is more interested in showing off, we need to find a way back to innovation ambition.*

We need to find our way back to thinking like the farmers mentioned in Chapter 3, rather than robber barons looking for the next thing to raid. Thankfully, there are signs that this is happening and that we're seeing new, fledgling seeds of another kind of innovation ambition. Y Combinator, the Silicon Valley accelerator par excellence, beloved by the innovation industry and home to many a me-too innovation over the years, announced in late 2018 that they wanted to invest into frontier technologies in carbon removal,[2] which represents something more than an accelerator getting into clean-tech. This is a signal that even Silicon Valley has started to experience innovation fatigue and realizes that something has got to change.

A bible of many in the shallow innovation space is *The Lean Startup*[3] by Eric Ries. It is undoubtedly a fine book on how to start a company, and Eric is a thoughtful young man who in conversation with me has stated some wariness towards those who create shallow or show-off startups. Still, the movement that has developed around it has been quite enthralled by the innovation industry. Yet here too are promising signals. A follow-up of sorts, with a foreword by Eric, is the new *Lean Impact*[4] by Ann Mei Chang, who argues that innovators should look for impact and 'radically greater social good' (as her subheading puts it).

Even the companies hailed by the innovation industry are getting in on the game. Apple is touting its credentials in sustainability and social responsibility. Companies in Palo Alto are debating the issues of inequality in a city where billions are made and the homeless are everywhere. And when Patty McCord from Netflix writes a business book, she calls it *Powerful: Building a culture of freedom and responsibility.*[5] So it seems care is making a comeback. Maybe the farmer didn't leave innovation, even if innovation for a moment left the farmer.

That said, we still need to work on our inner farmer. We need to work on care and respect and responsibility – for those we work with, for the world around us, for innovation itself. With this in mind, a quick return to some key points and then to the task ahead.

## The kit and caboodle, aka the whole shebang

*Repetitio mater studiorum est* – repetition is the mother of learning. As we are wrapping things up, a note about the core message of this book. If you want to build an innovation culture that shows resilience and defeats innovation fatigue, these are the things to keep in mind:

**The little things matter.** Yes, an innovation can die from something as tiny as a yawn. Yes, showing a little bit of respect to people can be an innovation engagement. A company's culture is not just built up out of fancy words on a website and a thrilling speech by a Chief Culture Officer, but also by the millions of subtle ways we treat each other and each other's ideas. It's not just the little things, but little things compound and can become a toxic goo that renders people unwilling to speak up and share and try. Big things are just little things accrued, and you can't expect to change the big picture if you're not prepared to work with the small one. (If you don't believe me, go back and re-read Chapter 2. Then we'll talk.)

**When it comes to ideas, it's nurture not nature.** In order to create a culture that values ideas, imagination and innovation, you need to pay attention to how people care about each other. This includes how they show respect to people and their ideas, how they take responsibility for the nurturing of ideas and how they reflect about their own role in all of this. Without a constant reciprocity, a give and take, you will never build a true innovation culture. It doesn't matter if you have people that can pump out ideas at the drop of a hat if you don't have a culture to support and nurture the same. (If this seems strange, go back and re-read Chapter 3. We'll wait for you.)

**Imagination beats everything.** All strategic failures are failures of imagination. The innovation industry says it's big on imagination, but this is a misunderstanding. It is big on the kinds of things it likes to call imagination, but it is mostly obsessed with celebrating what everyone else is celebrating and feeding back what it thinks its audience wants to hear. Real imagination is far more difficult and divisive and strange, and it is this specific thing that makes it so powerful. Particularly in an age of data and AI, imagination is the one true advantage we have. (If you disagree with this, go back and re-read Chapter 4. Or some poetry. Or maybe just go out and play.)

**Embrace diversity and the diversity of diversity.** If creativity and innovation are the engines of the modern economy, diversity is their fuel. We cannot have new thinking and new developments without a wide range of inputs, without the creative friction created when differences in opinion, knowledge, perspectives and experience meet. We don't need just one form of diversity, we need to respect and care for multiple diversities. And not just the diversity of people, but the diversities of the rhythms and tempos, the places and spaces of innovation. (If this seems overwrought, re-read Chapters 5 and 7. First one way, then backwards. First quickly, then slowly.)

*Purpose and ambition drive deep innovation.* We can innovate without really being too occupied with why, but the innovations we create in this way will always be shallow, pale things. They might make money, sure, but this does not in any way guarantee their overall impact will be positive. For the kind of deep, meaningful innovation that truly changes the world, we still need something more. We need a purpose, something that transcends motivational slogans like 'Innovate or die!' We need a grand ambition, the desire to do something that captures the immense cognitive surplus of ideas and innovation in our organizations and unleashes it on wicked, meaningful problems. In a very real way, we might need less but better innovation. (And if you don't agree, I'm not sure we can be friends. Also, you should re-read Chapter 6.)

## Why we need innovation critique

Some of my readers may have felt this book to be too critical. Some might think that I've been unfair to various innovators, and particularly that I've been unfairly critical of the diverse band of innovation consultants, authors and pundits I've called the innovation industry. Granted, I've not always been kind. But I contend that I have a right to be critical, and you do too! Innovation is too important to be treated with kid gloves, too valuable to be demeaned by being turned into nonsense and fairy tales. I also contend that it is in the best interests of innovation to criticize it. Not so that we seek to demolish it, perish the thought! But so that we keep honing it, and so that we can curb its sillier excesses. So that we can have not just more innovation but better innovation.

Also, as I come to the end of this book, which to a great extent has delved on problems in contemporary innovation – innovation fatigue, innovation nonsense, shallow innovation and so on – this might be a good place to outline a programme for progressing beyond improving a company culture. We live in a world that says it loves innovation, yet one that at the same time often opts for the easy solution, the quick buck, the shallow thrill. Innovation isn't easy or quick, yet we live our lives as if it were. We live in a world with no end to wicked problems: fake news, aging societies, growing inequality, excessive use of resources and a biosphere that may already be damaged past the point of no return.

In such a world, we need deep innovation more than ever. The kind of innovation that isn't done to get PR, or to impress a jaded business audience. The kind of innovation that aims for impact rather than yet another flavour of Pop-Tarts. Some still contend that innovation will get there on its own, in a strange recasting of trickle-down economics (you know, the theory that said that we'll all be better off if we just lower the taxes of the ultra-rich). I claim that innovation is guided by us and not just by our innovation engagements. Innovation is also guided by the way we talk about it, the way we criticize it (or choose not to), the values we either read or put into it. Innovation isn't just there, it is what we make it.

Innovation can change the world, but it cannot do so on its own. Innovation needs help, and sometimes, the best way to help is to critique. To highlight what is still good and true and valuable, and to point out what has become shallow, pointless and fatiguing. To speak plainly and truthfully about something, noting its flaws and foibles, not to put it down or denigrate it, but to help it be all that it can be. Today, too few criticize innovation, to its detriment. The one thing I hope this book has done is to

*Innovation can change the world, but it cannot do so on its own.*

encourage a few more people to criticize innovation, innovation talk and innovation thinking where it deserves to be criticized, whilst supporting and nurturing it where it needs it.

We need a broad societal dialogue about innovation, if it is to be all it can be. We need to hear from many different actors, not just the ones the innovation industry prefers. We need a discussion that is just as diverse and many-splendoured as innovation is. We need a discussion that talks about the purpose of innovation and about whether the resources we dedicate to it are intelligently used. We need to talk about innovation ambition and not just assume it is there.

If we start doing this, and if companies start doing this, we will have less innovation fatigue. We will have more meaningful innovation and stronger innovation cultures. It's too soon to tell if we'll manage to save the world with innovation. We might, as innovation is our best chance to do so, but we'll have to wait and see. And, whilst we wait, we can save our children from at least some inane innovation books and pointless innovation meetings, and that's always something.

# Notes

## Chapter 1

1  This figure can be reached in a number of ways. I used the simplest one, to ascertain a baseline, and used the advanced search functions for Amazon.com. Searching, in late 2018, for books that have innovation in the title and have been published after 2014, you get more than 7,000 results, i.e. no less than 117 books for each month. Granted, some of these will be reprints, new editions and the like, but one needs to keep in mind that Amazon only stocks some languages – my own book in Swedish, entitled 'Innovation' isn't counted amongst the 7,000+ titles listed. Assuming that the amount of books written on innovation in e.g. Swedish, other European languages, Russian, Chinese, various Indian languages, etc offsets the number of false positives in this list, the figure of 100 books a month seems reasonable (if still insane). It might even be a lowball estimate.

2  As quoted in DuBois, L (2011) *Soccer Empire: The World Cup and the future of France,* University of California Press, Berkeley, CA, p. 79

3  For the Strategy& report, see Jaruzelski, B, Staack, V and Goehle, B, eds (2014) Global innovation 1000: Proven paths to innovation success, *strategy+business*, 77, n.p. For the BCG report, see Wagner, K, Taylor, A, Zablit, H and Foo, E, eds (2014) The most innovative companies 2014: Breaking through is hard to do, in *Report from the Boston Consulting Group*, Boston Consulting Group, Boston, MA

4  See Fast Company [accessed 27 November 2018] *The 50 Most Innovative Companies in the World* [Online] www.fastcompany.com/most-innovative-companies/2018

5  Berman, D [accessed 27 November 2018] Is a Peanut Butter Pop-Tart an Innovation? *The Wall Street Journal* [Online] www.wsj.com/articles/SB10001424052702304854804579236601411310502

6  Stanley-Bostitch [accessed 3 March 2013] Stanley-Bostitch® Office Products/Amax Incorporated Revolutionizes Classroom Pencil, Press release [Online] www.bostitchoffice.com/press/detail.php?id=9

7 For one of the few academic treatments of innovation fatigue, see Chung, GH, Choi, JN and Du, J (2017) Tired of innovations? Learned helplessness and fatigue in the context of continuous streams of innovation implementation, *Journal of Organizational Behavior*, **38** (7), pp 1130–148. Note, however, that they primarily discuss innovation fatigue as arising from failed projects.

8 This is a setting in a Tesla that allows the car to accelerate in an incredibly rapid and not all that safe manner. It has in later models been referred to as 'Ludicrous mode' – and can take the car from 0 to 60 mph in 2.9 seconds. Which is a bit of a show-off.

9 For an example, see e.g. Rockman, S [accessed 27 November 2018] How Apple Killed Innovation, *Forbes* [Online] www.forbes.com/sites/simonrockman1/2018/04/23/how-apple-killed-innovation/

10 Barsh, J, Capozzi, MM and Davidson, J (2008) Leadership and innovation, *McKinsey Quarterly*, **1**, 37–47

11 Shirky, C (2010) *Cognitive Surplus: Creativity and generosity in a connected age*, Penguin, Harmondsworth, UK

12 In Vance, A [accessed 27 November 2018] This Tech Bubble is Different, *Bloomberg Businessweek* [Online] www.businessweek.com/magazine/content/11_17/b4225060960537.htm

13 See OECD Data [accessed 27 November 2018] *Gross Domestic Spending on R&D* [Online] https://data.oecd.org/rd/gross-domestic-spending-on-r-d.htm or consult the global R&D funding forecasts from the Industrial Research Institute, available at iriweb.org. Also see the report from the National Science Board [accessed 27 November 2018] *Science & Engineering Indicators 2018* [Online] www.nsf.gov/statistics/2018/nsb20181/

14 Baird, R (2017) *The Innovation Blind Spot: Why we back the wrong ideas – and what to do about it*, BenBella Books, Dallas, TX

15 Negroponte, N [accessed 27 November 2018] Big idea famine, *Journal of Design and Science* [Online] https://jods.mitpress.mit.edu/pub/issue3-negroponte

16 See e.g. Morozov, E (2013) *To Save Everything, Click Here: The folly of technological solutionism*, PublicAffairs, New York

17 Erixon, F and Weigel, B (2016) *The Innovation Illusion: How so little is created by so many working so hard*, Yale University Press, New Haven, CT

18 Gordon, RJ (2017) *The Rise and Fall of American Growth: The US standard of living since the civil war*, Princeton University Press, Princeton, NJ

19 In private conversation, but see also Catmull, E and Wallace, A (2014) *Creativity, Inc: Overcoming the unseen forces that stand in the way of true inspiration*, Random House, New York

## Chapter 2

1 See Hollister, R and Watkins, M (2018) Too many projects, *Harvard Business Review*, **96** (5), pp 65–71

2 See Nove, A (1958) The problem of 'success indicators' in Soviet industry, *Economica*, **25** (97), pp 1–13; also Hanson, P (2014) *The Rise and Fall of the Soviet Economy: An economic history of the USSR 1945–1991*, Routledge, Oxford, UK

3 For more on this, see Gladwell, M [accessed 27 November 2018] Creation Myth: Xerox PARC, Apple, and the Truth About Innovation, *The New York Times* [Online] www.newyorker.com/magazine/2011/05/16/creation-myth

4 For a take on this, see Detert, J and Burris, E (2015) [accessed 27 November 2018] Nonverbal Cues Get Employees to Open Up: Or Shut Down, *Harvard Business Review* [Online] https://hbr.org/2015/12/nonverbal-cues-get-employees-to-open-upor-shut-down-2

5 Wilson, JQ and Kelling, GL [accessed 27 November 2018] Broken Windows: The Police and Neighborhood Safety, *The Atlantic* [Online] www.theatlantic.com/magazine/archive/1982/03/broken-windows/304465/

6 For an interesting counter example, however, see Graeber, D (2018) *Bullshit Jobs: A theory*, Simon & Schuster, New York

7 For more on this, see Rehn, A (2011) *Dangerous Ideas: When provocative thinking becomes your most valuable asset*, Marshall Cavendish, Singapore

8 Moon, Y (2010) *Different: Escaping the competitive herd*, Crown Business, New York

9   See e.g. CNN [accessed 27 November 2018] Ryanair's 5 'Cheapest'
     Money-saving Schemes [Online] https://edition.cnn.com/travel/article/
     ryanair-money-saving-schemes/index.html
10  See, Carlsberg Group [accessed 27 November 2018] Somersby Was
     the Fastest Growing of the Global Top 10 Cider Brands in 2012
     [Online] https://carlsberggroup.com/news-archive/somersby-was-
     fastest-growing-of-the-global-top-10-cider-brands-in-2012/
11  See e.g. Steve Blank's blog post [accessed 27 November 2018] How
     to Avoid Innovation Theatre [Online] https://steveblank.
     com/2015/12/08/the-six-critical-decisions-to-make-before-
     establishing-an-innovation-outpost/

## Chapter 3

1   Edmonson, A (1999) Psychological safety and learning behavior in
     work teams, *Administrative Science Quarterly*, **44** (2), pp 350–383
2   See e.g. Duhigg, C [accessed 27 November 2018] What Google
     Learned from Its Quest to Build the Perfect Team, *New York Times*
     [Online] www.nytimes.com/2016/02/28/magazine/what-google-
     learned-from-its-quest-to-build-the-perfect-team.html
3   Porath, C [accessed 27 November 2018] Half of employees don't feel
     respected by their bosses, *Harvard Business Review* [Online]
     https://hbr.org/2014/11/half-of-employees-dont-feel-respected-by-
     their-bosses?autocomplete=true
4   Porath, C (2016) *Mastering Civility: A manifesto for the workplace*,
     Grand Central Publishing, London
5   Cowan, R, Sanditov, B and Weehuizen, R (2011) Productivity effects
     of innovation, stress and social relations, *Journal of Economic
     Behavior & Organization*, **79** (3), pp 165–182
6   Grant, AM (2014) *Give and Take: Why helping others drives our
     success*, Penguin, Harmondsworth, UK
7   Brown, B (2015) *Daring Greatly: How the courage to be vulnerable
     transforms the way we live, love, parent, and lead*, Penguin,
     Harmondsworth, UK
8   David, S (2016) *Emotional Agility: Get unstuck, embrace change
     and thrive in work and life*, Penguin, Harmondsworth, UK

# Chapter 4

1 Magee, C [accessed 27 November 2018] The Age of Imagination: Coming Soon to a Civilization Near You, *Second International Symposium: National Security & National Competitiveness: Open Source Solutions (Vol. 1)* [Online] www.oss.net/dynamaster/file_archive/040320/4a32a59dcdc168eced6517b5e6041cda/OSS1993-01-21.pdf

2 See McGrath, RG, van Putten, AB and Pierantozzi, R (2018) Does Wall Street buy your growth story? For how long? *Strategy & Leadership*, **46** (2), pp 3–10

3 Kahneman, D (2011) *Thinking, Fast and Slow*, Farrar, Straus and Giroux, New York

4 I should here note that I've been inspired by the work of Nancy Brennan and her 'Hierarchy of Imagination', although it was also the ascending theme and lack of resistance in her schemata that made me question similar representations.

5 This very fancy word means the one chapter before the penultimate one. That fancy word means the one before the last. Yes, I love both words and get to use them too rarely.

6 Gino, F (2018) The business case for curiosity, *Harvard Business Review*, **96** (5), pp 48–57

# Chapter 5

1 Chang, E (2018) *Brotopia: Breaking up the boys' club of Silicon Valley*, Penguin, Harmondsworth, UK

2 Interestingly, the frequency-hopping system she designed that later led to e.g. WiFi, was developed in collaboration with the composer and pianist George Antheil, adding one more layer of diversity to the mix.

3 See, for instance and as tasters, the following articles. Rock, D and Grant, H [accessed 28 November 2018] Why Diverse Teams Are Smarter, *Harvard Business Review* [Online] https://hbr.org/2016/11/why-diverse-teams-are-smarter; Hewlett, SA, Marshall, M and Sherbin, L [accessed 28 November 2018] How Diversity Can Drive Innovation, *Harvard Business Review* [Online] https://hbr.org/2013/12/how-diversity-can-drive-innovation

4   Walter, I (2011) *Steve Jobs: A biography*, Simon & Schuster, New York
5   Baird, R (2017) *The Innovation Blind Spot: Why we back the wrong ideas – and what to do about it*, BenBella Books, Dallas, TX
6   Hunt, V, Price, S, Dixon-Fyle, S and Yee, L (2018) *Delivering Through Diversity*, McKinsey, New York
7   Reynolds, A and Lewis, D [accessed 28 November 2018] The Two Traits of the Best Problem-Solving Teams, *Harvard Business Review* [Online] https://hbr.org/2018/04/the-two-traits-of-the-best-problem-solving-teams
8   Reynolds, A and Lewis, D [accessed 28 November 2018] Teams Solve Problems Faster When They're More Cognitively Diverse, *Harvard Business Review* [Online] https://hbr.org/2017/03/teams-solve-problems-faster-when-theyre-more-cognitively-diverse
9   See e.g. Rosso, BD (2014) Creativity and constraints: Exploring the role of constraints in the creative processes of research and development teams, *Organization Studies*, **35** (4), pp 551–85; Dayan, M, Ozer, M and Almazrouei, H (2017) The role of functional and demographic diversity on new product creativity and the moderating impact of project uncertainty, *Industrial Marketing Management*, **61**, pp 144–54
10  Jang, S (2017) Cultural brokerage and creative performance in multicultural teams, *Organization Science*, **28** (6), pp 993–1009
11  Regarding Uber, see e.g. Smith, NC and McCormick, E (2019) Uber and the ethics of sharing: Exploring the societal promises and responsibilities of the sharing economy, in *Managing Sustainable Business*, eds Lenssen, GG and Smith, NC, pp 579–611, Springer, Dordrecht, the Netherlands. Regarding WeWork, see Brown, E [accessed 28 November 2018] WeWork: A $20 Billion Startup Fueled by Silicon Valley Pixie Dust, *Wall Street Journal* [Online] www.wsj.com/articles/wework-a-20-billion-startup-fueled-by-silicon-valley-pixie-dust-1508424483
12  AARP [accessed 28 November 2018] The Longevity Economy [Online] www.aarp.org/content/dam/aarp/home-and-family/personal-technology/2016/09/2016-Longevity-Economy-AARP.pdf
13  See Centers for Disease Control and Prevention [accessed 28 November 2018] Global Diarrhea Burden [Online] www.cdc.gov/healthywater/global/diarrhea-burden.html

# Chapter 6

1   Frankfurt, HG (2009) *On Bullshit*, Princeton University Press, Princeton, NJ

2   Spicer, A (2017) *Business Bullshit*, Routledge, London

3   Christensen, CM (1997) *The Innovator's Dilemma: When new technologies cause great firms to fail*, Harvard Business School Press, Boston, MA, p 15

4   Blacksocks™ [accessed 28 November 2018] [Online] www.blacksocks. com/int/en/socks/calfsocksblack-plus

5   Graeber, D (2018) *Bullshit Jobs: A theory*, Simon & Schuster, New York

6   OK, so this is a joke, but it's also a reference to a previous note about the innovation mindset in a medtech company I once worked with; see Chapter 1.

7   EY [accessed 28 November 2018] Why Business Must Harness the Power of Purpose [Online] www.ey.com/en_gl/purpose/why-business-must-harness-the-power-of-purpose

8   Harvard Business Review Analytic Services [accessed 28 November 2018] The Business Case for Purpose [Online] https://hbr.org/ resources/pdfs/comm/ey/19392HBRReportEY.pdf

9   Sinha, S [accessed 28 November 2018] Stanford Educated Ratul Narain is Helping Babies Battle Hypothermia with a Simple Bracelet, *YourStory* [Online] https://yourstory.com/2016/04/bempu/

10  See Stokes, PD (2005) *Creativity from Constraints: The psychology of breakthrough*, Springer, Dordrecht, the Netherlands

11  See e.g. Baer, M and Oldham, GR (2006) The curvilinear relation between experienced creative time pressure and creativity: Moderating effects of openness to experience and support for creativity, *Journal of Applied Psychology*, **91** (4), pp 963–70

12  Pederson, CL and Ritter, T [accessed 28 November 2018] Great Corporate Strategies Thrive on the Right Amount of Tension, *Harvard Business Review* [Online] https://hbr.org/2017/11/great-corporate-strategies-thrive-on-the-right-amount-of-tension

13  Ibid.

14  DiMaggio, P and Powell, W (1983) The iron cage revisited: institutional isomorphism and collective rationality in organizational fields, *American Sociological Review*, **48** (2), pp 147–60

15  Groysberg, B, Cheng, Y-J and Bell, D [accessed 28 November 2018]
    2016 Global Board of Directors Survey [Online] https://c.ymcdn.com/
    sites/www.womencorporatedirectors.com/resource/resmgr/
    Knowledge_Bank/WCDBoardSurvey2016_FINAL.pdf
16  For a good overview on individual resilience in an innovation
    context, see Moenkemeyer, G, Hoegl, M and Weiss, M (2012)
    Innovator resilience potential: A process perspective of individual
    resilience as influenced by innovation project termination, *Human
    Relations*, **65** (5), pp 627–55

## Chapter 7

1  See e.g. Virilio, P (1986) *Speed and Politics: An essay on dromology*,
   Semiotext(e), New York
2  See e.g. Arthur, C [accessed 28 November 2018] Nokia's Chief
   Executive to Staff: 'We Are Standing on a Burning Platform', *The
   Guardian* [Online] www.theguardian.com/technology/blog/2011/
   feb/09/nokia-burning-platform-memo-elop
3  Coyle, D (2018) *The Culture Code: The secrets of highly successful
   groups*, Bantam Books, New York
4  Heath, C and Heath, D (2017) *The Power of Moments: Why certain
   experiences have extraordinary impact*, Simon & Schuster, New York
5  Dodgson, M and Gann, D [accessed 28 November 2018] The Missing
   Ingredient in Innovation: Patience, World Economic Forum [Online]
   www.weforum.org/agenda/2018/04/patient-capital/
6  Sleep.org [accessed 28 November 2018] Five Companies That
   Encourage Power Napping [Online] www.sleep.org/articles/5-
   companies-encourage-power-napping/
7  Before cheap and efficient photocopying, armies of secretaries copied
   business papers in 'typing pools'.

# Chapter 8

1   Rosenthal, R and Jacobson, L (1968) Pygmalion in the classroom, *The Urban Review*, **3** (1), pp 16–20

2   Piper, K [accessed 28 November 2018] Silicon Valley Wants to Fight Climate Change with These 'Moonshot' Ideas, *Vox* [Online] www.vox.com/future-perfect/2018/10/26/18018454/silicon-valley-sam-altman-yc-climate-change-carbon-moonshot; also see carbon.ycombinator.com

3   Ries, E (2011) *The Lean Startup: How today's entrepreneurs use continuous innovation to create radically successful businesses*, Crown Books, New York

4   Chang, AM (2018) *Lean Impact: How to innovate for radically greater social good*, John Wiley & Sons, Hoboken, NJ

5   McCord, P (2018) *Powerful: Building a culture of freedom and responsibility*, Missionday, Arlington, VA

# Index

Note: Numbers, acronyms and 'Mc' within main headings are filed as spelt out.
Page locators in *italics* denote information contained within a figure or table.

United States (US) 79, 139–40
unlearning 90–92

values 64
velocity 168–70
vulnerability 84, 85–87

*Wall Street Journal* 7
WeWork 138
World Economic Forum 177

Xerox (Xerox PARC) 37–38
Xerox 914 177–78

Y Combinator 193
yawning 38, 39, 41, 46, 49, 63, 69,
    72, 194

Zimbardo, Philip 42–43